THE SEXUAL PERSON
The Church's Role in Human Sexual Development

By Urban T. Holmes III   PROFESSOR OF PASTORAL
THEOLOGY,
NASHOTAH HOUSE

IN COLLABORATION WITH

Henry R. Olivier   PSYCHIATRIC EXAMINER
DIOCESE OF LOUISIANA

AND

Warren Breed   FORMER PROFESSOR
OF SOCIOLOGY,
TULANE UNIVERSITY

THE SEABURY PRESS · NEW YORK

THE SEXUAL PERSON: THE CHURCH'S ROLE
IN HUMAN SEXUAL DEVELOPMENT
was prepared under the auspices of the
Executive Council of the Episcopal Church.

Scripture quotations, unless otherwise noted, are from the *Revised
Standard Version of the Bible*, copyrighted 1946 and 1952 by the
Division of Christian Education, National Council of Churches.

FOREWORD

THE study you hold in your hands is the result of about seven years of reading, reflection, conversation, writing, and testing on the part of a number of concerned adult churchmen. In 1963, at a meeting of the Department of Christian Education of the Diocese of Louisiana, a number of people shared with the whole group their uncertainties in working with youth, particularly as related to problems of sexuality; for we were just beginning to feel the impact of the so-called sexual revolution. There seemed to be little information to guide us, and we felt the need for research and explication of the Church's approach in this area of life.

The result of this first cry for help was a committee appointed by the Department of Christian Education, which began to work through its assignment—to clarify what is healthy sexuality and how it may be developed in youth—by assigning, writing, and discussing a series of position papers. The commitment, the openness, and the hard work of that group—sometimes to very late hours—was a source of deep satisfaction. The basic approach and shape of this book was hammered out in that committee, although only a small part of the original work is contained herein. A number of names no longer appear as contributors, but they deserve a large share of what credit there may be: Robert J. Dodwell, then diocesan director of youth; Thomas C. Aycock, then chairman of the Adult Division of the Department of Christian Education; William M. Smith of the School of Education, Louisiana State University in Baton Rouge, and at a somewhat later date, the Ven. Willis R. Henton, the Archdeacon for Christian Education of the Diocese of Louisiana.

This does not by any means describe everyone to whom we owe initial thanks. The original report was shared first with the whole Department of Christian Education and then became the substance of a clergy conference of the entire Diocese of Louisiana. Although we would not want to imply that all or any of the people then involved necessarily accepted the opinions expressed even in the first form of the study, we do owe them a debt for their willingness to reflect on this material and talk with us about it.

The publication of the first study was widely used in programs throughout the diocese, and from the reactions there—and to some extent elsewhere—we discovered that we were meeting a definite need. In the process of working through the subject, we came to certain convictions that others found helpful, and these convictions are what we offer in the pages that follow. We had no brief at the beginning except our deep concern; but in time we concluded that before we could talk about sexual morality we had to discuss the theology of sex; and before we can begin to educate the youth, we must seek to re-educate the adults. Therefore, this study is principally an explication of a theology of human sexuality and an appeal for acceptance by adult churchmen.

Since 1964 there has been a spate of material—religious and secular—on sex. Some of it is very good, and this material is included in the Bibliography. Some other is not worthy of comment. The one thing we had yet to discover, however, was a clear statement of the basic thesis of our findings. For that reason, in 1968 the Diocese of Louisiana issued a revised edition of the study. It consisted largely of the evolution of the general editor's own thinking, in the light of continued reading, pastoral experience, and reaction to the initial offering by clergy and laity. Aside from many interested and receptive churchmen, young and old, with whom the ideas found here were discussed—particularly the enthusiastic young people at conferences at Camp Hardtner near Pollock, Louisiana—there were a number of persons who figured prominently in the dialogue. Ernest F. Bel, until recently assistant headmaster at St. Martin's School, Metairie, Louisiana, and Robert M. Cooper, then the assistant chaplain at Louisiana State University in Baton Rouge, are two whose caliber gives hope for the Church in the future.

Certain adjustments emerged and were carried further in this final form. There was a tempering of the logic as a result of the experience of pastoral application, a deepened conviction of the truth of the basic premises, and an expansion of the application of the theological position. There was also a serious effort to update the material. In working through the first revision and in developing the final form, the original committee was not consulted and responsibility for the few deletions, additions, and reinterpretations is mine.

Perhaps the most notable change from the initial draft is to be found in the chapter on "Sex Education and the Church." Recently, sex education has come into its own and has, at the same time, become rather controversial. My own experience is that where clergy and lay leaders are not afraid of sex education, they are seeking guidance in its implementation. In this chapter our intention is to clarify some rather gross misconceptions about sex education and provide a context from which church leaders can intelligently proceed.

In working out the final draft, I have had the opportunity for further dialogue with students, colleagues, and occasional experts, and once again new insights were gained. I treasure the subtle and, alas, occasionally heated conversations with my fellow faculty member, Thomas Talley. His mark is to be found in chapter 1. The Rev. Roy Turner, rector of St. Luke's Episcopal Church, Bethesda, Maryland, and the Rev. Peter Stone, rector of St. Matthew's Episcopal Church, Kenosha, Wisconsin, have provided solid clinical experience. My students in "Sex, Marriage and the Family" have cleared up many a point in debate. And I am particularly indebted to Alan Bell, senior psychologist of the Institute for Sex Research at the University of Indiana, who read the manuscript at a late stage and gave it his "imprimatur."

The intended audience for this study is the concerned adult, clergy or lay person, who is seeking a reasoned approach to human sexuality. We do not claim that ours is the only tenable position for the Christian, and we hope no attempt will be made to apply this "easy" label to our work. To some we will undoubtedly appear quite conservative. We believe there is such a thing as human nature, and we argue from both a natural and a revealed theology. Our comments are quite freely laced with moral conviction. To others we will seem very liberal. We advocate sex education and the possibility that every sexual act cannot be judged solely on the basis of a marriage license. Our hope is to avoid categories and labels. There is, we believe, no simplistic prescription for sexual behavior; not "anything goes as long as you're concerned," nor "it's the nasty prelude to babies." Obviously, we believe that to be human is to be a *sexual person*, and that this is good and something to be enjoyed. But what does it mean to be a "sexual person"? In what ways does this shape our behavior? How do we develop healthy patterns of sexuality? Is there any hope in our society for this kind of sexuality? What is the

Church's role in teaching the sexual person? These are the kinds of questions we are trying to answer in what is offered here.

Beyond the individual reader, we have no one particular use of the study in mind. It has already found a place in some seminary and college courses, and we hope that the Christian education committees of our parishes will give it close examination. It is intended as a stimulus, source, and guide for parochial and interparochial programs in this area. It can become preinvolvement reading for small groups studying human sexuality, leading them into a consideration of the central issues of the subject. We also hope it will have a strong influence upon the thinking of those charged with the responsibility for the national church's study of sexuality.

The book may appear to be rather heavily documented for a semipopular work, but there are good reasons for this. For one thing, there is the editor's compulsion to give credit for ideas that are not strictly his own. For another, there is the attempt to take a specific position—which, in fact, has its controversial elements—and the reader has the right to know when this is purely our own speculation and when it can be supported from other sources. Finally, this work is only one small contribution to a vast field of study, and it is hoped that the reader will pursue the subject further in specific and in general areas of interest.

One concrete criticism of the study has been the obvious omission of any discussion of homosexuality. The reason for this can be explained historically. It was hoped that the Diocese of Louisiana, following upon this examination of heterosexuality, would authorize a further investigation of homosexuality. That investigation never came to pass, but the national church now has such a study underway. We do think there are obvious implications for a study of homo-

Evelyn Hooker!

sexuality from what we say here, particularly in the light of chapter 1. As much as we believe in treating the committed, overt homosexual as a person, we cannot help but conclude that his behavior is in contradiction to what it means to be a sexual person. This is the conclusion to which H. Kimball-Jones comes in *Toward a Christian Understanding of the Homosexual*,[1] * which is a most compassionate little book. I would recommend that the interested layman start with this. If he is further worried about homosexuality and family life, he might consult Peter and Barbara Wyden, *Growing Up Straight*.[2] Beyond this he can wrestle with the works of Martin Hoffman, Stanley Willis, Irving Bieber, Gore Vidal, and Wainwright Churchill.[3]

It would be most ungrateful to omit offering a word of love and appreciation for those whose interest, patience, and confidence made all this possible. Our wives, of course, but even more our bishops. The Rt. Rev. Girault M. Jones was always willing to give us free rein, as well as to finance our deliberations; and the Rt. Rev. Iveson B. Noland was most generous with his time and listened and counseled with us constantly. We hope their investment in us draws some reward.

URBAN T. HOLMES

Whitsuntide 1969

---

* Numbers in text refer to Reference Notes at the back of the book.

CONTENTS

THE SEXUAL PERSON
The Church's Role in
Human Sexual Development

* I *

A THEOLOGY OF SEX

IF ANY discussion of sexual morality is to make sense, it must begin with an ontology of sex—some perception of the role of sexuality in human nature. Too often the Church and its spokesmen have been party to efforts to impress upon our youth the necessity for chastity on the grounds of expedience, failing to see its paradigmatic quality for the total interpersonal life.

Some years ago Margaret Mead, churchwoman and anthropologist, wrote: "I believe that the real issue about premarital sex is the risk of producing illegitimate children." This concept is indefensible from the Church's point of view, for if medical science can guarantee that coitus is possible without any risk of conception (as it may well do soon if it has not already), then reason for premarital continence is destroyed.

Also indefensible is the view of coitus as fundamentally, if not exclusively, for the purpose of procreation. This concept is contrary to a Biblical understanding of the purpose of coitus.[1] *

Even less defensible are reasons for chastity based on so-called double-standard appeals to masculine pride: that men want to marry virgins, but feel no obligation to remain chaste themselves.

We must broaden our view of sex. Derrick S. Bailey, an outstanding theologian in this field, makes the very important point that too often we equate the word "sex" with

* Numbers in text refer to Reference Notes at the back of the book.

1

actual sexual intercourse or coitus. This places a limitation upon our idea of sex and makes impossible any discussion of its true significance, which is far broader and much more profound than coital behavior, interest, or pleasures. He insists that "the scholar at least should endeavor as far as possible to restrict the unqualified use of 'sex' and 'sexual' by relating them strictly to the *being* of Man, and not to his behaviour or biological functions." [2] Because this use of the words "sexual" and "sex" is so adverse to the common practice, other authors employ the word "gender" to refer to Man's masculinity and femininity and let the more popular terms stand for his physiological or biological dimensions.[3] Since we believe it is essential to keep a clear distinction between the discussion of Man's anatomical conformations and his very being (for reasons that shall be made clear as we progress), we shall use the words "coitus" and "sexual intercourse" for the physical act, and reserve any references to "sex," "sexuality," and "gender" for the nature, or ontology of Man.

I. MAN AS A SEXUAL PERSON

If we are going to develop such an ontology, we must take note of the Christian Doctrine of Creation; particularly the creation of Man. The basic statement of all Biblical anthropology is: "Then God said, 'Let us make man in our image'" (Genesis 1:26). This is the reflection of a sophisticated Jewish theologian, writing about the fifth century before Christ. The "man" to which he refers is generic Man, and does not refer to gender.[4] To distinguish this usage we shall capitalize the word "Man" throughout this article when we mean it in a generic way.

The author of this part of Genesis continues in the next verse to explain what he means by this statement. "So God created man in his own image, in the image of God he created him; male and female he created them" (1:27). The words "male" and "female" may be seen as correlative terms intrinsic to Man. To be human is to exist in a masculine and feminine complementarity, and without this Man is incomplete. As Derrick Bailey says of this verse: "It implies even in this Old Testament context that human sexuality is something more than adaptation for generation—that it has, in fact, a metaphysical import."[5]

It seems reasonable to assume that, to the mind of the author of Genesis 1:27, the image of God in Man is closely related to human sexuality. "In the image of God he created him; male and female he created them." The late Karl Barth, one of the most influential theologians of our century, considers this a significant insight into the meaning of the image of God. "Men are simply male and female. Whatever else they may be, it is only in this differentiation and relationship. This is the particular dignity ascribed to the sex relationship."[6] When we say this we carry the vexed question of the precise meaning of the image of God back to a reflection upon the nature of the male and female roles. In a society in which so much has been done to obscure such an understanding, as Harvey Cox so aptly points out in *The Secular City*,[7] it is important that we explore theological thought that transcends the popular notions of our times.

Nicolas Berdyaev, an early twentieth-century theologian of the Eastern Church, offers a similar insight. He writes: "As the image and likeness of the Creator, man is creator too and is called to creative cooperation in the work of God."[8] We would add to this that one cannot think of the role of creation without relating it to the capacity to love. Here, love means the free offering of self to the end that God's purpose in creating the object of love might be fulfilled. To love, then, is to cooperate in God's creative act.

This particular understanding of the nature of the image of God in Man is essential to a grasp of the Christian ontology of Man upon which we would base a theology of sex. Of course, it requires that our understanding of Creation itself be not static but a dynamic process of becoming. God creates *now*, not just at some distant date in the past. Therefore, Man has the opportunity to be a real partner in the process of creation. His love is not simply a poor reflection of the divine love. He is a channel of the living love of God, working through him as a free instrument to bring about the fulfillment of God's Creation.[9]

This brings us to assert that the power of cooperation in creation, which is the image, is expressed in human sexuality. "In the image of God he created him; male and female he created them." But here again our conception of gender, male and female, is often confused if not distorted. We speak generally of "male characteristics" and "female characteristics" in what amounts to a very careless manner, failing to really distinguish between what is of the essence of masculinity and femininity and what is simply an idea or prejudice imposed by our particular culture or society. The common sort of distinction, frequently expressed, is seen in the ancient Hebrew. There the word for man is *'ish*, coming from a root meaning "strong"; and the word for woman is *'ishshah*, which is derived from a root meaning "soft" or "delicate." [10]

Such socially imposed distinctions, Bailey says, "are generally quite arbitrary, and never universal or unvarying—though some are relatively widespread and enduring; but they always indicate the sexual ideas of a culture, and reflect or produce both true and false notions of sex." [11] It is important to note, furthermore, that whatever feminine and masculine characteristics we may isolate in fact or fantasy, they are never discovered in an absolute form in a given individual. Here we can profit from Carl Jung's seemingly mysterious discussion of the *anima* and *animus* in every person.[12]

Yet there is a difference between the sexes, or our discussion would mean nothing (see Appendix at end of chapter). While it is important that for pastoral reasons we must not be deluded by false notions of sexual difference, at the same time we need to have a clear picture of where the distinction lies. Erich Fromm, in an essay on this subject, states that while the similarity between man and woman is greater than the dissimilarity, it is possible to distinguish a fundamental ontological difference: the function of the male requires that he be assertive, and that of the female demands that she be the willing recipient.[13] Berdyaev makes a more philosophical distinction when he says: "The masculine principle is essentially personal and anthropological. The feminine principle is essentially communal and cosmic. It is only the union of these two principles that constitutes a complete human being." [14] He would seem to mean by this that the masculine principle is that of the individual actively coming to a realization of the meaning of himself as a person, while the feminine principle is the willing acceptance of the relationship of individual to individual and of Man to the totality of Creation and Creator.

Sociologists William Simon and John Gagnon offer a helpful discussion of this point in an article, "Psychosexual Development," in *Trans-action magazine*. In the male, they say, there is a developmental movement from a predominantly genital sexual commitment to a loving relationship with another person. But this movement is, in effect, reversed for females, with love or affection often a necessary precondition for intercourse.[15] This insight is perhaps not startlingly new, but it is good to have scholars of such reputation document it. What it says can be translated to reveal that for the male, aggressive satisfaction is primary, and for the female, relationship comes first.

Biblical support for all this is to be found in several sources. In the earlier account of man's creation the formation of woman is explained: "It is not good that man should be alone; I will make him a helper fit for him" (Genesis 2:18). Cole says of the passage, "Woman . . . is the doorway into community." [16] Schillebeeckx quotes Lagrange, "Woman is man's vis-à-vis." [17] (We must be very sure not to try to force this kind of distinction upon individual men or women, however; there is, even biologically, a feminine factor in every man, and vice versa.[18]) In Genesis 2:24 occurs the text quoted by both our Lord (Matthew 19:5; Mark 10:7) and the author of Ephesians 5:31: "Therefore a man leaves his father and mother and cleaves to his wife, and they become one flesh." Perhaps it has not occurred to some that in the marriage rite the movement of bride to groom—the woman is *given to* the man —is inconsistent with this verse. Of course, this marriage rite is taken from pagan Roman customs, which express the legal status of women; namely, as chattel. While there seems to be some uncertainty about the exact status of women in Judaism in pre-Christian times, it would appear that a theology of sexuality prevails over any theory of property rights. Then again, the Biblical analogy of Israel as the bride of God (Hosea 2:19–20) and the Church as the bride of Christ (Ephesians 5:21–33) seems to underline this same concept of the individual (masculinity) in relation to community (femininity).

At the risk of simplifying an idea to the point where its real meaning becomes obscured, we will say that in human sexuality there is the potential of a creative interrelationship between Man's need for inner self-realization and his need for the support of the creation outside of himself. It is in the process of coming to see the meaning of his own person, while at the same time being responsive to his place in an interdependent community of creation, that Man (i.e., in both sexes) comes into being.

Referring once again to the familiar verse quoted by our Lord in St. Mark's Gospel—"For this reason a man shall leave his father and mother and be joined to his wife, and the two shall become one"—we find here the most clear expression of the role of sexuality in the creative order. Scholars speak of this as a concept of *henosis* (from the Greek word for "one"). Derrick Bailey describes *henosis* as "the resolution of discord, the transcending of superficial differences and antagonisms at a new or deeper level of existence or experience; not an amalgamation in which the identity of the constituents is swallowed up and lost in an undifferentiated unity, nor a mere conjunction in which no real union is involved." He goes on to speak of it as an "organic" (could we say ontological?) union, and concludes by saying: "This means that through the sexual intercourse in which they consummate their love they restore the original pattern of human unity." [19]

Otto Piper, a pioneer in the theology of sex, obviously considers *henosis* a central point. He attributes three meanings to it. First, this teaching maintains that the life of two people is changed into what it was not before. Second, it is a unity of man's physical and mental life where the presence or absence of the other party determines "the course of all the processes of life." Third, it is a union that once achieved cannot be dissolved into the prior state, as is physically symbolized in the child which is the result of the mutual coital union of the two people. [20]

Thus, the personality created in this *henosis*, the object of human sexuality, is complete Man; in the sense that

"God made Man." In a given man or woman there is a partiality, an incompleteness, that is only resolved in the union of man and woman to achieve Man. "The two shall become one." The fulfillment of the capacity of human sexuality, therefore, would seem to play a vital role in the whole matter of holiness, understood as *wholeness of being*. It would suggest that "you have to be married to be saved." It is important that we examine in what sense this might be true.

good

Can we support this statement? In the face of some New Testament testimony and a good bit of Christian thought through the centuries, it is rather extreme. Remember that the emphasis is on *wholeness of being*, a balanced fulfillment of all that is potentially Man. In this light Piper makes the point that "because sex is indispensable for God's plans of salvation, only compelling reasons, such as are included in God's redemptive purpose, can dispense us from the duty of marriage." [21] Piper uses sex sometimes to mean coitus, and there is some confusion resulting from this. But understanding the more general meaning for the word "sex," Piper's statement that "sex is indispensable for God's plans of salvation" is correct. Furthermore, sex is generally fulfilled in coitus, and therefore it is generally true that all of us have a duty to marry. But failure to marry does not necessarily deny us sexual fulfillment (and in all fairness to Piper, he goes on to say this in a different manner). When we are physically or emotionally impotent, or when for reasons beyond our control there is no one whom we may marry, as well as when we live a celibate life for the sake of exercising a more effective ministry, there is still the possibility of expressing our sexuality in a noncoital manner. This is extraordinary, and often takes extraordinary courage; but it is possible. Therefore we should not be too ready to laugh at the priest who says, "I am married to the

Church," or the nun who speaks of our Lord as her spouse. We must have something more than hope of a future marriage to offer the unmarried who seek the Church's counsel.

It is in this context that we might make reference to a subject often delicately avoided and likely to arouse considerable emotion; namely, the sexuality of our Lord. Our attitude on this subject can be an accurate barometer of our freedom from a latent Manichaeism. The sexuality of Jesus was the subject of a recent article by Tom Driver, republished in *New Theology No. 3*.[22] He observes quite accurately that "a sexless Jesus can hardly be conceived to be fully human."[23] But at the same time, if we are to assert that our Lord was without sin, as the author of Hebrews says in assuring us that He was also fully human, we would naturally assume Him to be among those who expressed their sexuality in an extraordinary manner, as opposed to a coital expression. This is not to propose that Christ was without temptation, such as *Kazantzakis* describes in *The Last Temptation of Christ*; for we are not docetists. Nor am I inclined to accept the thesis of G. Wilson Knight, in *The Christian Renaissance*, who makes of Jesus an androgynous creature, unlike any human before or since. To the best of our knowledge our Lord was never married, and therefore, assuming premarital coital activity to be of a probable sinful nature (and this will be discussed more fully later), we would presume the necessity for a non-venereal outlet for His sexuality.

II. SEXUALITY AND SACRAMENTALITY

Yet, when all this has been said, it remains true that marriage is the normal channel for the expression of human sexuality, because coitus is the normative sacramental expression of human sexuality. It becomes necessary to say why this sacramental act of coitus needs to be confined to marriage (the Church is too often inclined to say it is without explanation, hence youth's rebellion), but first we need to review a significant part of sacramental theology.

Sacramental theology rests upon the belief that God is creator of all the world, and that this creation is an act of love. "And God saw everything that he had made, and behold, it was very good" (Genesis 1:31). We must constantly remind ourselves of this truth. None of us are ever safe from the appeal of Manichaeism, with its deceptively easy solution for the problem of evil. We mean the tendency to erect a dualism between "spirit" and "matter" that is parallel to "good" and "evil." In such thinking, the solution to materialism is to despise the material world; the answer to alcoholism is prohibition; and "sex (coitus) is nasty" *per se* because of the tragedy of fornication, unwed mothers, and adultery. This identification of sin with the thing itself incites a certain guilt even within the most sophisticated Christian. None of us is exempt completely from the Puritan syndrome, which H. L. Mencken defined as "The haunting fear that someone, somewhere, may be happy." It is, of course, a heresy, a blasphemy against the Doctrine of Creation, which teaches that God's world of spirit and matter is an indissoluble unity.

We must, therefore, be most careful that in teaching on the subject of sex we never create the impression that we are postulating some sort of separation between the spiritual world and the material world. We must begin with a doctrine of Man that clearly states that because we are single organisms which can be characterized as both spiritual and material, there is no possibility of living in either realm without involving the other.

Of course, the most profound testimony to this doctrine

is the Incarnation itself. We remind ourselves that God became Man as well as *a man* (as we have just indicated) in the full sense of the word—physically as well as spiritually. The history of Christian thought is cluttered with individuals and groups who have attempted to water down this fact, but the Catholic Church has rightly resisted any attempt to remove the scandal of a God who assumes human flesh. For we recognize that if Man be restored to that wholeness for which God has made him, it must be by means of his total life—physical as well as spiritual.

From this it follows that human creativity, in terms of spiritual sexuality, must also involve physical sexuality. There is no arbitrary separation between the two. If we agree with what men like Berdyaev say in abstract terms, we must also realize that it is in terms of coitus that this becomes a reality in the lives of human beings. The physical is inseparably involved in the spiritual reality.

Furthermore, coitus is not simply the expression of a union of male and female into one person that already exists. In other words, it is not simply the sign of the *henosis* that has been previously established upon some "mystical plane." *It is, on the contrary, the chief means whereby this union is in fact achieved.* It is constitutive of the marital bond, as the Eucharist is constitutive of the Christian community. There is value in saying that, properly used, coitus can be an instrument in developing a closer bond between a man and his wife;[24] and as St. Paul says (I Corinthians 7:3–6) there is an obligation within marriage to have a regular and reasonably frequent pattern of sexual intercourse.

This is not to say that coitus exhausts the sacramental implications of marriage. Obviously, there is a physical sharing in the use of a common house, common money, common hopes, common food, common sufferings and in the relationship to common children. But nowhere is this commonality found to express such a profound depth of union as it does in the act of sexual intercourse. It is here that, if we permit, the sense of union that comes to its fulfillment in the whole Man is experienced in its fullest. Therefore, while it is certainly true to say that "sex (coitus) is not everything in a marriage," it is certainly a point of reference without which all the other experiences of the marital union become dissociated one from the other. Coitus can be said to be not unlike the Eucharist in that, although not the totality of Christianity, it is to our mind the *sine qua non* of a full religious life.

From what has been said, we can sum up our discussion of the sacramental implications of sex by observing that we cannot separate the spirituality—the *eternal* implications of human sexuality as man's creative capacity—from the very physical and particular act of coitus. The latter is the sacramental means of effecting the true end of human sexuality, the whole Man.

III. The Nature of the Sexual Union

With this said, we may turn to the question of sexuality as it relates to marriage. Perhaps again we need to remind ourselves of a fact or two. Principally, we do not confuse the reality of marriage with the liturgy of matrimony itself. In the marriage liturgy the ministers of the sacrament are, of course, the Christian man and the Christian woman. The matter and form of the sacrament is the promise of a lifelong commitment between them before witnesses.[25] The function of the clergy and the marriage liturgy is to afford a right setting for this to be initiated, and to give the blessing of the Church to the marriage. But it is not by virtue of the fact that the prescribed liturgy of the Church was followed that this is a marriage. It is rather the combination of two qualified people joining together in clear consent to an indissoluble union that is the heart of the matter. It is in the light of this that we might think about the role of human sexuality.

In the Old Testament we find what is often wrongly considered a mere euphemism for sexual intercourse: the verb "to know." "Now Adam knew Eve his wife, and she conceived and bore Cain" (Genesis 4:1). This sort of expression is also found in classical Greek literature. It indicates an insight into what happens in sexual intercourse that we, in our supposed sophistication on matters of sex, frequently miss.

Essentially there are two ways of speaking of "knowing" something. The classical discussion of these two ways is to be found in the thought of Martin Buber, modern Hebrew philosopher and theologian, who distinguishes between *I–Thou* and *I–It*.[26] These may be understood as the knowledge of an object, in which the knower does not involve himself personally in the thing known; and as the knowledge of a person as person, in which there is a mutual encounter and involvement of the knower and the person known. This second kind of knowledge, Piper rightfully points out, cannot be communicated to someone outside the immediate experience. You cannot tell someone how you love your wife so that they can view the relationship with the same existential involvement as you.[27]

The I–It relationship in the area of human sexuality is most clearly recognized in a man's coitus with a prostitute. This encounter of two individuals in what is physically the most intimate experience people know, is not only devoid of any desire for real meeting, but care is taken that there be none. It is not uncommon, for example, for a prostitute to express revulsion at the thought of kissing a client, because this would express in her mind a form of affection and concern for the other *as a person*. At the same time there is no pretense on the part of the client but that she is a *thing*, simply an object of his sensual pleasure. Of course, the real truth is that coitus cannot lend itself to a simple I–It relationship.

For sexual intercourse necessarily exposes two individuals to the knowledge of one another characterized by the I–Thou relationship. Even in the most callous coital act there is an element of honesty, in which the mask slips, and the true self is revealed to the partner. Though a man would leave all but his physical self at the bedroom door, he cannot—not even at the door of a prostitute. As he reveals his physical self, so indeed is his total self unveiled and made vulnerable. He is exposed not only physically, but emotionally and spiritually. The ego boundaries dissolve. In a sense, he is at the mercy of his partner as in no other relationship.

This is hard for some people to grasp, yet it may well be the great original contribution of St. Paul to the understanding of human sexuality. Recall his words, often ignored or misunderstood, in which he says: "Do you not know that he who joins himself to a prostitute becomes one body [*soma*] with her" (I Corinthians 6:16). Barth's commentary on this verse, as well as on Ephesians 5:31 ("For this reason a man shall leave his father and mother and be joined to his wife, and the two shall become one [*sarx*]"), makes the point:

Both *sarx* and *soma* denote more than the physical body. Therefore, the expressions about the two being one flesh and body do not merely imply their physical union in itself and as such . . . they go much further and denote the whole man as a psycho-physical being which is established, animated and sustained by the spirit. And if two human beings become one flesh or body, while this does also express their physical union, beyond this it denotes the union of their total being to total and indissoluble fellowship.[28]

Bailey offers essentially the same opinion: "Intercourse therefore is much more than a mere physical act which takes place in the periphery, as it were, of personal experience; it involves the whole man and the whole woman in the very center and depth of their being, so that afterwards neither can ever be as if they never came together. This is true even of fornication." [29]

Difficult as it may be for some to see, this is what lies at the heart of St. Paul's and the Church's opposition to premarital or extramarital sexual intercourse. After all the sentimentality has been thrown over the reality of the situation, coitus requires by its nature the disclosure, as Piper puts it, of the "inner secret" of the self.[30]

The only thing that can support this kind of self-disclosure is the total commitment of the person. In I–Thou there is the possibility of the most beautiful sort of creative relationship, but it requires the unconditioned self-offering of the lover to the beloved, not only at that moment but in the totality of their life. This is because you cannot separate the moment of coitus from the mutual daily relationship to which it is the climax. The ideal is certainly, then, that this surrender of self to the other which we describe as love is not limited in any way. It is not limited by time: "I love you in September, but not in December"—or space: "I'm all yours in New York, but I'm Susie's in Chicago."

In a more subtle way, love is not limited in the eventualities of the act of coitus. We cannot isolate sexual intercourse in some kind of absolute manner from conception, physically (the pill is not for everyone and the best of the others—intrauterine device, diaphragm with jelly, etc.— have a 2 per cent failure rate), emotionally, or theologically.

There is, we would believe, in the over-all coital relationship an urge to project this union into progeny, which has theological roots in the Old Testament. If an "accident" or unconscious intention that creates a pregnancy is going to destroy the relationship between the couple, then it would appear that the union might be held in question from the start. As a matter of fact, is there not something lost in any sexual relationship that fails to enjoy coitus either in anticipation of children or in thanksgiving for those already in the next bedroom? This is to say that we subscribe to the "principle of totality," a concept that is vigorously condemned in *Humanae Vitae* and yet commonly held in Anglicanism. This concept maintains that whereas every marital relationship to be true to itself must intend and actively seek procreation, nonetheless family planning and consequent use of contraception is not only permissible but also a positive good.

When this total commitment is *not* present, then the self-revelation that comes necessarily in sexual intercourse will most probably be destructive of the relationship of both people involved. Piper, speaking of such a situation, describes something he calls "sex honour" which he considers innate in a woman and acquired by a man in his proper sexual relationship with the other sex. The term "honour" is probably too much misunderstood, but Piper seems to mean the sense of integrity found in true sexual acceptance. With this understanding he is quite right when he says, "If a man robs a girl of her honour . . . , he loses his own honour." [31] Despite all youthful protestations to the contrary, when total commitment to one another is lacking or not possible, coitus is ultimately selfish; the partner is being "used." The sense of personal integrity that is found in the proper coital relationships is lost, and the only alternative is that we see ourself and our partner as *things*.

This is to take the so-called hard line. Having made this statement, I want to modify it in several ways. First of all, I must acknowledge that such a "total commitment" as a reality truly existing between two people is more likely to be an ideal than an unqualified fact. Even in marital sexual relationships of a satisfactory kind there is always a destructive element, though we would hope it is slight. "Total commitment" is something emotionally dubious and inaccessible to psychometrics. This may appear to dismiss lightly the earnest claim of some theologians to the truly "redemptive" quality of a rare coital alliance before or outside marriage. For example, J. A. T. Robinson defends the relationship described in *Lady Chatterley's Lover* as "in a real sense something sacred, as in a real sense an act of holy communion."[32] The evidence usually offered for redemptive premarital and extramarital relations is often, like this, of the literary kind. Yet I think occasional clinical material crops up, where there is real indication that an individual has come to a greater sense of identity as male or female, and has therefore come to understand himself or herself in God's purpose better, as a direct result of coitus outside marriage.

I recall the case of an unmarried woman in her midthirties, who in counseling with me spoke of a life of fear and uncertainty through her twenties. She came to know a young man, went with him for some time, and they engaged in a regular pattern of sexual intercourse. She could look back on this relationship as having awakened her to herself *as a woman*. In the face of all my probings, she insisted that she was grateful for what had happened and suggested that her impending marriage to another man could be anticipated without fear as a result of this previous experience.

Another case study, mentioned to me by a pastoral counselor of considerable training and skill, involved a teenager exhibiting psychotic symptoms. Her developmental history was quite traumatic, and she had a pattern of promiscuous behavior. However, it appeared that the only circumstances under which she could maintain a reasonable freedom from depression was when she engaged in sexual intercourse. I surmise that in this experience there was a discovery of some sense of identity, and she was able to cope with her inner anger. The counselor simply observed: "I am not sure that we can legitimately say that her sexual activity contributed to this, but neither am I sure that it did not." [33] The point is that we have to maintain an open mind.

This need can be illustrated further in a different setting by some clinical material recently published in two studies of the previously married, either widows or divorcees. Bernadine Kries and Alice Pattie cite cases where they believe sexual intercourse between the death of the previous spouse and remarriage were a creative way of handling this critical period of transition.[34] Morton Hunt in his study of the divorcee believes there are love affairs that are truly restorative, bringing about a "revaluation of oneself as a love object." [35] We might accuse them of fuzzy thinking or of failure to take seriously the revealed law; but it is probably best to allow the possibility of the truth of these claims, realizing that the immediate sense of discovery must be judged over the long course of events, and that even then much will always remain unknown.

Erik Erikson, undoubtedly a leading figure in adolescent psychoanalysis today, makes the suggestion that every person seeking maturity needs a "psychosocial moratorium." He defines this period as a time of experimentation, "a span of time after they have ceased being children, but before their deeds and works count toward a future identity." [36] Since the two primary nuclei about which identity structures cluster are the vocational and the sexual, there seems to be some ground for speculation about the possibility that in some rare instances actual coital experience is almost inevitable before identity can be established and a person can move on to the possibility of intimacy.

In *After Auschwitz,* Richard Rubenstein has something to say on the subject of premarital sexual intercourse that we would do well to consider. He makes the point that most such activity known to him is extremely neurotic, but he is unwilling to make a blanket condemnation of all such behavior. He says: "In sex the real question is: Are we prepared for that level of intimacy in dealing with another person?" [37] He seems to imply that this is not frequently the case, and I would agree.

If I offer this modification to what originally appears to be a very hard saying, it is only to remove it from the realm of "black and white" where no true morality can exist (much as the insecure might wish it could). Certainly the creative power of coital engagement is greater as the possibility of total commitment is greater. Therefore, most premarital, and almost without exception all extramarital venereal behavior, is undoubtedly sinful, because it is more destructive than otherwise. [38] Some marital intercourse is also sinful for the same reason. There is, as we shall see, no guarantee in a wedding ceremony.

The main burden of our thesis, although faced with certain rare exceptions, receives some support in a study by Kirkendall, entitled *Premarital Intercourse and Interpersonal Relations.* In this sociological appraisal of 200 case studies he offers, by implication and by what he leaves unsaid, some indication that there is pragmatic evidence of what we maintain here. He says, for example:

Some deeply affectionate unmarried couples have, through the investment of time and mutual devotion, built a relationship which is significant to them, and . . . experience intercourse without damage to their total relationship . . . it seems that in practically all instances 'non-damaging' intercourse occurred in relationships which were already so strong in their own right that intercourse did not have much to offer toward strengthening them.[39]

In other words, "marital type" of commitment was already there. Of course, we are led from this point to reflect briefly on the honest inquirer who, while admitting the need for a commitment in sexual relationships at the moment, sees neither the value of the marriage service in securing this commitment nor any reason why Man cannot observe consecutive or successive polygamy.

The purpose of this paper is not to argue the latter point in detail, but only insofar as it involves human sexuality. The basis of any answer to this would concern the nature of the sexual *henosis*. We do not see how we can treat it as purely a matter of legal contract without doing great violence to our Lord's teaching in St. Mark 10:2–12.[40] There is an irrevocable quality in the kind of commitment that human sexuality requires. If, then, *henosis* is not simply contractual, it must be in some sense ontological. It is of the nature of existence as God has made it. This would seem to us the only sense in which to understand, "What therefore God has joined together, let no man put asunder" (Mark 10:9).

Of course, there are those who protest against this on pastoral grounds. "Why punish people for a previous mistake?" Piper, a Presbyterian, answers: "Marriage attains its true end only if it is monogamous," [41] and this excludes successive as well as concurrent polygamy. For once the "secret of sex" is shared outside of the unique encounter of two people, it cannot be shared with another in the same sense. Interestingly enough, Bailey, an Anglican, does not take such a rigid stand and bases his discussion of this problem on love as the ontological basis of *henosis*. He feels that it is inaccurate to speak of marriage as indissoluble, because when love dies it does dissolve. He considers the Scriptural authority subject to interpretation in the light of the contemporary scene to which the authors spoke, and he would suggest repentance as the only basis of marriage after divorce.[42]

To my mind, Piper's argument combines a certain Biblical intransigence with an appeal to the emotional reaction say, of a second wife wondering if her husband enjoys coitus more with her than he did with his first wife. Yet Bailey is not at all clear in calling love the "ontological" basis of *henosis*. For such love appears to be no more than a moral quality and leaves us with a rather weak marital "cement." His Biblical exegesis, as well as his treatment of the "Solemnization of Holy Matrimony" in the Book of Common Prayer, appears a rather tedious and unconvincing effort to support a conclusion to which he feels he must come. Perhaps the only realm in which this question can be resolved is in the reality of *henosis* in a given marriage, and that once it has become a fact it is indeed indissoluble. This would mean that we do need a deeper appreciation and a wider use of the concept of nullity—not as a ruse but as an honest recognition that the marriage service can be an unwitting farce. At the same time, however, we would do better to encourage the heroic witness to the purpose of human sexuality in the order of creation. This says far more for the dignity of the image of God within Man than the implied editing of the marriage service to read "until death of love does us part" (as we understand has been done). Here "love," I suspect, is often no more than infatuation.

What does this say about the "Solemnization of Holy Matrimony" in the Book of Common Prayer? Certainly we would not advocate that the witness to the holy wedlock of two Christian people be made anywhere other than in the context of the Church's liturgy. Yet it is even more unthinkable for a couple, neither of which is Christian by fact or intention, to be married "in the Church" simply for sentimental reasons or for purposes of social convenience. Indeed, it is a moot point whether or not we are justified in asking a non-Christian—marrying a Christian—to make the assumptions required of one participating in the Church's rite of Holy Matrimony.

The rite itself is not of the *esse* (necessary for the very existence) of marriage. From the Christian point of view it is perhaps more of the *plene esse* (necessary for a complete or full understanding) of marriage. This can be illustrated in the light of the tradition that marriage is a Sacrament only between two Christians; that is, the manifestation of the sacred in historical visibility. Between non-Christians, it would be maintained, it is a natural act, apparently incapable of receiving that "supernatural" power bonding a man and woman together into a lifelong union.[43] Yet when a non-Christian couple are baptized, their marriage, *ipso facto*, becomes a Sacrament.[44] It would be then safe to assume from even this point of view that it is not the fact that a marriage is performed by the rite of the Church that makes it a Sacrament; but that two Christians by their own will, together with the power of God, desire to complete a Christian marriage that makes it a Sacrament.[45]

Historically, this can be readily seen. In the early Church a Christian marriage was witnessed by a blessing and the offering of the Eucharist. The actual espousal well up into the Middle Ages was handled by laymen.[46] In the Eastern Church this is still symbolized by the fact that the espousal is held at the church door, and only the "coronation" within the church proper. The famous Roman

Catholic liturgical scholar, Duchesne, sums up the practice of the Church for the first thousand years this way:

> No ecclesiastical law obliged Christians to seek a blessing on their marriage. It was a matter of custom or propriety, and although it subsequently became the rule, it was never a condition of validity. The marriage is independent of the rite.[47]

Considering that the Church did not decide finally that marriage was a Sacrament until the eleventh century, this sort of attitude is even less surprising. Probably most influential in its final decision in favor of matrimony was not any profound understanding of human sexuality, but the rather specious exegesis of Ephesians 5:31–32 in the Vulgate: *"Propter hoc relinquet homo patrem et matrem suam, et adhaerebit uxori suae, et erunt duo in carne una. Sacramentum magnum est."* ("On account of this a man leaves his father and mother, and is united to his wife: and two are in one flesh. It is a great sacrament.") *Sacramentum* becomes in Christian theology a technical word, but as such it is far too narrow a translation for *mysterion* (from the original Greek text), which can simply mean a "mystery" in the common sense of the word; although *mysterion* is also the Greek word for sacrament.

In view of all this, one caveat needs to be made. What we have said should not be taken to mean that we believe the social recognition of the marriage is unimportant or even unnecessary. Marriage has an essential relationship to society; it is in almost all cultures the agency of socialization, and this is a vital and responsible function.[48] Therefore, the society has a stake in the marriage and the marriage in society. To be a whole person is not only to possess an interpersonal self, but a social or cultural self as well.

IV. IMPLICATIONS

The point has been reached at which we must draw all this together and ask what it might mean for us as Christians. Truth that lacks meaning is without value, in that it possesses no power for our lives. The underlying conviction of this chapter is that everything said is of great value, and the chapters that follow seek in part to explicate this for us all. Basically, there are at least four implications here for us:

First, to be human is to live as a *sexual person*. We cannot isolate coitus from the totality of life. It is not a peripheral activity of our life, requiring only a momentary pause in the mainstream of an essentially asexual existence. We are not just occasionally sexual and at all other times sexual ciphers. No matter what our venereal behavior might be—promiscuous, marital, or celibate—we engage the world in terms of masculinity and femininity. Creative living is contingent upon our grasp of our sexual identity, both intellectually and emotionally.

Second, the meeting of two people, if it is to convey a transforming power, is essentially sacramental. This follows naturally from an Incarnational theology of the type that lies behind this chapter. The intimate physical contact of coitus is not different *in kind* (it is, of course, *in degree*) from all sorts of physical contacts that are appropriate to varied forms of relationships; it is, rather, the most profound expression of the deepest love we know between two people. All love of one person for another is rightly expressed by the appropriate gift, touch of a hand, or kiss.

Third, an absolute juridical or simple contractual view of marriage and sexual intercourse misses the subtle psychological and sociological forces at work in sexual encounter.

The creative power of sexuality culminates in a coital relationship expressive of near total commitment; but we can never be absolutely certain of the existence of this. Those of us for whom lack of control is a source of panic can find this frightening, but mature judgment requires that we take it into account in formulating a theology of sex and marriage.

Fourth, an ethic that succumbs to the impulse of the moment, or to a sentimental rationalization of premarital or extramarital coitus, does not take human nature seriously. There is a great depth to Man; and when we fail to exercise the *total person*—our rational faculties as well as our feelings, our social responsibilities as well as our immediate interpersonal setting—in decision-making, we are certainly not fulfilling the image of God within us. As a matter of fact, we may be courting disaster.

It should now be obvious, from what has been said, that sex is not peripheral to human existence. Much less can we allow the "virtual identification of coitus with sin or evil" as found in the thought of St. Augustine of Hippo.[49] Human sexuality is a vital factor in the creative process of God, from which emerges the whole Man. It is only natural to expect that such a power, with its tremendous potentiality, be equally liable to the danger of disastrous misuse. The complete answer to the destruction wrought by its constant abuse does not lie, however, in more education in the physiology of sex, important as that may be, or in a casual attitude toward what is essentially mysterious, but in a profound sense of the high place of man and his role in God's plan of creation. This is to repeat our opening declaration that a theology of sex must rest upon an ontology. Human sexuality lies at the center of human existence, and can only be understood in the light of the answer to the question: "What is Man?"

APPENDIX TO CHAPTER 1: "A THEOLOGY OF SEX"

We are not unaware that our bald statement on page 5
—"Yet there is a difference between the sexes. . . ."—is
highly controversial, particularly when it is related, as it is
here, to basic human nature. For the person who holds this
in question, or who would like to pursue the issue further,
a survey of some of the arguments from a theological point
of view may be found in Urban T. Holmes, "A Theology
of Gender," *Journal of Pastoral Care*, Vol. 23, No. 4 (December 1969), pp. 218–226. Some of the basic works that
might be read and that argue against a theory of ontological
gender differentiation include: Simone de Beauvoir, *The
Second Sex* (New York: Bantam, 1968); Abel Jeanniere,
The Anthropology of Sex (New York: Harper & Row,
1967); and Mary Daly, *The Church and the Second Sex*
(New York: Harper & Row, 1967). Anne Anastasi, "Psychological Differences Between Men and Women," *Women
in Modern Life*, ed. William C. Bier, S.J. (New York:
Fordham U. P., 1968), pp. 42–54, is helpful; as well as the
article by William Simon and John Gagnon, "Psychosexual
Development," *Trans-action—Social Science and Modern
Society* Vol. 6, No. 5 (March 1969), pp. 9–17. For those
positions favoring some sort of gender identity rooted in
human nature, we would recommend: Karl Stern, *The
Flight from Woman* (New York: Farrar, Straus & Giroux,
[Noonday] 1965); Vance Packard, *The Sexual Wilderness*
(New York: McKay, 1968); and Charles Winick, *The
New People: Desexualization in American Life* (New
York: Pegasus, 1968). Winick's book is a little speculative
to be entirely convincing. Research by geneticists, biochem-
ists, and medical doctors in this field is also helpful. From
personal conversation with Dr. James F. Crow of the Uni-
versity of Wisconsin, we are familiar with genetic research

that indicates a positive correlation between the biological anomaly of XYY chromosomes (called Klinefelder's Syndrome) and those incarcerated for crimes of violence or aggression. The theory is that there might also be a positive correlation with professional football players. John Money, "Influence of Hormones on Psychosexual Development," *Medical Aspects of Human Sexuality*, Vol. 2, No. 11 (November 1968), pp. 32–42, introduces us to the wonders of androgen in its capacity to differentiate the male fetus as well as to induce aggressive sexuality when administered to the postpubescent female. Perhaps most interesting of all is some research being done at the medical school at Marquette University, where an attempt is being made to actually work out an objective scale of sexuality on the basis of eye movement. It has already been proven that this is different in masculine and feminine persons: E. H. Hess, "Pupillometric Assessment," *Research in Psychotherapy*, Vol. 3 (1968), pp. 573–583; E. H. Hess *et al.*, "Pupil Response of Hetero- and Homosexual Males to Pictures of Men and Women," *Journal of Abnormal Psychology*, Vol. 70 (1965), pp. 165–168; B. B. Beck, "The Effect of the Rate and Intensity of Auditory Click Stimulation on Pupil Size," (unpublished paper, 1967); and R. A. Hicks *et al.*, "Effects of Pupil Size and Facial Angle on Preference for Photographs of a Young Woman," *Perceptual and Motor Skills*, Vol. 24, No. 2 (April 1967), pp. 388–390.

In our recent correspondence with Dr. Allen Bell, senior psychologist of the Institute for Sex Research at the University of Indiana (the so-called Kinsey Institute), Dr. Bell noted that too many theories of sexuality forget that Man has a body. We would not only agree with this but point to its theological meaning and insist that a theology that does not take into account a body that differentiates the sexes is inadequate.

2

PSYCHOLOGICAL FACTORS IN CURRENT SEXUAL BEHAVIOR

WITHIN the past two decades it would appear to many in the psychiatric profession that American moral standards have undergone a wrenching change.[1] This is nowhere more evident than in the sexual behavior of adolescents and young adults. It is no longer possible to predict or evaluate this behavior by prewar standards, as there has evolved a generation of young people who show no continuity with the next oldest group. It has been said that there is more than one generation's difference between the current generations. Indeed, the author and many others in a pastoral responsibility believe that the young people of today took as a starting point in their moral structure a position so at variance with the previous standard that there is no connection between the two.

Some clergy have shown an alarming tendency to ignore, overlook, or otherwise deny what is actually happening within and among their youth. Many parents and other responsible adults join them in this ostrichlike stance. This is the most dangerous approach to the problem, for it reinforces what we believe to be a highly significant cause of the sexual behavior of today's youth. We cannot detach ourselves from the problem with the remark: "Maybe others do this, but our young people certainly don't!"

Some observers have become alarmed at the increase in venereal disease, especially syphilis, not only in the general population but especially among teenagers.[2] There has been

28

noted an absolute (i.e., irrespective of population increase) increase in illegitimate births in the past 25 years.[3] It can be argued that illegitimacy, venereal disease, etc., have been present in our society all along. We agree. It is not the presence of such phenomena that causes concern, it is their alarming increase.

Most probably, there are multiple factors implicated in the change in American moral structure. Increased mobility of family members through automobiles might be one. The current rise in the standard of living has had less definable but perhaps equally important effects on the national character.

However, since this portion of the report deals with psychological factors affecting sexual behavior, we would like to pose this question: Given two adolescent couples with the same dating habits, opportunity, and freedom, why will one couple engage in increasingly intimate sexual behavior terminating in regularly practiced intercourse, while the other will not engage in intercourse, though they may engage in very heavy petting? Since the external factors—the use of a car, attendance at various planned or unplanned functions, etc.—are the same, we must look for an *internal* difference in the two couples. By this we mean a difference in the mental makeup of these couples that says to one pair "far enough" and says nothing to the other boy and girl.

Psychologically we would say that this limiting "voice" that our chaste individuals hear comes from that part of the mind called the superego. This organ of the mind is developed from the individual's ego (or is that portion of the mind which attempts to achieve a balance between external and internal reality limitations and which is only partially conscious; that is, is only partly accessible to direct contact with the ego).

culture 'tells'

The superego may be said to largely resemble what we call the individual's conscience. Ernest Jones says: "We have good grounds for supposing that to the activity of the superego we are mainly beholden for the imposing structure of morality, conscience, ethics, aesthetics, religion— in short to the whole *spiritual* [italics added] aspiration of man that sunders him most strikingly from the beast. The well-nigh universal belief that man is qualitatively different from other animals in possessing a divine and immortal soul itself emanates from this source." [4] It is the repository for parental injunctions against various kinds of behavior; societal norms, as interpreted by the parents and passed on to the children; religious beliefs and tenets learned by the child through exposure at home and at church; cultural values as demonstrated by the parents; and finally peer-group mores and behavior patterns learned from playmates. The superego also contains positive learnings and injunctions, such as it is good to save, to be honest, etc. We add this to emphasize that the superego is not only a prohibiting force in a negative sense, but also a positive, encouraging force toward those aspects of behavior that the individual was taught were good.

The reader will note that the bulk of the learning that constitutes the superego comes from the parents. This is undoubtedly true in any individual's *early* life. Learning from peers or other adults will only take place on a large scale if the parents are either physically or psychologically absent from their task. (It is our belief that the latter situation is most prevalent in our culture today.) It is in the years from 7 to 20 that completion of the learning process and development of a well-functioning superego is solidified, and the individual is prepared for the psychological tasks involved in negotiating puberty and young adulthood.

There is no abrupt point at which an individual begins

formulation of his superego or conscience. Its rudimentary structure is seen as early as 18 to 24 months. There should be a definite well-functioning superego by school age. During the grammar school experience, firmer crystallization of this psychic entity takes place, so that the individual has some solid backing when he enters adolescence.

As this brief survey attempts to show, much of the behavior, good and bad, shown by adolescents and young adults has its origin in earlier developmental phases. These phases are further drastically influenced by the behavior of the older segments of society that the child observes. That is, the development of the individual under the guidance and example of his parents is of primary importance in determining future behavior patterns of all types. Emphasis should be placed on the example of behavior to which the growing child is exposed. Chaotic lives in the parents lead to chaotic lives in the children. Less striking, but no less important, are the parents who fail to furnish any particular example, either good or bad, for their children. In these cases the young people are forced to find examples from their peers or other adults.

The group with which this paper is most concerned is the adolescent and young adult population. For our purposes we will define this age group as extending from puberty to the firm establishment of "adult identity" and role.

Adult identity involves many factors and is not easily defined. Erik Erikson uses the term "ego identity" to denote the crystallization of a "lifelong development largely unconscious to the individual and to his society. Its roots go back all the way to the first self-recognition: in the baby's earliest exchange of smiles there is something of a *self-realization coupled with a mutual recognition*" (Erikson's italics).[5] When the individual achieves conscious self-realization and this is, in turn, validated by the mode in which society reacts to him, a formation of "ego identity" may be said to have taken place. Thus a juvenile truant who sees himself as such and is treated by society (the juvenile court) as such may be said to have achieved an ego identity, although a faulty one.

During late adolescence the struggle to achieve an ego identity leads to what Erikson calls "ego diffusion" and a loss of much of what had previously been gained through identification and introjection of parent and parent-surrogate models. The resultant "crisis" leads to adolescent disturbances of many sorts. In an attempt to solidify themselves around some type of object relationship, many adolescents turn to sexual behavior.

One of the major features and problems that must be resolved by the adolescent is a revival of the Oedipal conflict. The characteristic features of this situation (carnal desire for the mother, jealousy and hatred for the father, fear of castration, etc.) are of supreme importance in the development of the superego (see above). Indeed Freud termed the superego the heir of the Oedipus complex. If a satisfactory resolution to this conflict is reached in early childhood, with a superego neither too weak nor too powerful, there is a repetition and strengthening of the superego structure, and the individual proceeds to other tasks.

Conversely, if there is not a satisfactory resolution at the earlier stage, a repetition of the failure recurs and the defect in the superego is reinforced. The added complication is that now the individual is capable of physically mature expression of the superego conflict, in aggressive behavior, sexual or physical violence, vandalism.

It would appear that many of today's adolescents and young adults have a severe defect in their superego structure that lends itself to premature expression of intimate, physical, sexual behavior.

It should be remembered also that the adolescent ego has but recently emerged from the struggle with aggression and its sublimation in interpersonal situations. This is the so-called latency effort; that is, the work of that period of life from the end (or temporary cessation) of the Oedipal conflict period to puberty. In the case of many adolescents, the question may be authentically raised as to the success of the latency effort. Unsolved aggressive drives, left over from the latency period, combined with sexual feelings and stirrings, may lead to "acting out;" that is, to conscious external expression of the aggression in a sexual mode. This is harmful to the individual and frequently to others.

If, in addition, the individual's ego structure is weakened by the latency effort, with or without success of said effort, there may be insufficient strength left to deal with the increased demands pubery places upon the ego. Also, if the ego receives insufficient "support" from the superego in dealing with the erupting sexual strivings from the unconscious, it may give in to these demands for expression of the sexual drive to relieve internal psychic tension (e.g., masturbation, coitus, petting leading to orgasm) and thus ward off serious mental disturbance.

One of the most important manifestations of ego strength at this particular period is the individual's ability to accept and act within *the reality principle*. This states that one gives up immediate gratification that might be accompanied by pain (in the broadest psychic sense) in favor of future gratification without pain.

We trust it is obvious from our previous discussion that for a given individual's ego to be able to utilize the reality principle he must have developed internal controls or limits (the "inner voice" of our adolescent couple, above). These limits rest in the superego and are not consciously or directly heard as a "voice." Nevertheless, the individual perceives the limit, and directs his conscious behavior accordingly. As we said above, the developing child learns control through limitation of his behavior by his parents, or by the parents positively fostering what they consider "good" behavior. This begins as early as the toilet training period, and Ferenczi speaks of "sphincter morality," indicating how early limitation of behavior begins.[6]

For parental limits to be successfully internalized, however, they must be *clearly stated, repeated, emphasized, reinforced, and rewarded.* Above all they must be *consistent.* The parents cannot be divided as to where the limits are set, nor can a parent verbally say one thing and give tacit permission for another. There must be no doubt in the child's mind of the personal consequences of his behavior in any given area.

Communication between parents and children must begin early in the child's life. Limits cannot be presented in the manner necessary for learning without it. Without communication at an earlier age there can be none later, as the parents and children, by the time adolescence will have occurred, will have grown further and further apart.

Internalization of limits is fostered by the fact that limits offer the developing individual a sense of security and assist him in dealing with the anxiety inherent in coping with his unconscious impulses.

All of the above may be applied to the adolescent, as he is in as desperate a need of security and limits as the preschool child, really even more so.

Besides contributing to their internal representation in the superego, consistent presentation of limits aids in developing the individual's *self-concept.* This may be thought of as a complementary portion of the identity of the individual as discussed above. *The self-concept of an individual is in large part a reflection of the way he has been treated by the significant people in his life.* It is as if the individual says to himself: "Well, at least they care (love, respect) enough about me to be concerned with what I do and how I do it."

The self-concept of any adolescent has great influence on the mode and extent of sexual expression that the individual will allow himself or herself. The well-worn cliché of the "nice girl with whom you don't go too far" is actually an expression of that girl's self-concept reflected by another's behavior (as amplified in chapter 3).

Thus we see that an individual's self-concept, identity, ego functioning, and superego development are intimately linked to the type and amount of interaction and communication first with parents, then with parent-surrogates, especially in the area of presentation of firm, consistent limits on behavior. (These limits also take the form of consistent approbation of "good" behavior. The two modes of reinforcing this learning are really inseparable.)

It is further obvious that this lays the responsibility squarely on the parents. It is the basic contention of this paper that much, if not all, of the premature sexual behavior evidenced by the adolescent of today results from a failure of formation of the moral and ethical aspects of the individual's superego (self-concept) identity. Since this is primarily the responsibility of the parents it is imperative that they be given some aid and assistance in this critical role.

The parents of the average teenager today may well have superego defects themselves. At the very least, however, it cannot be denied that they cannot communicate to their children what it is they *do* believe. Because of the gap that exists between generations today, direct communication is extremely difficult. We know of no better currently existing means to bridge this gap than the Church. Here both parties may be brought together on common ground, the Faith, and may have clearly interpreted to them what is their obligation to the Church and to each other. Parents need authoritarian support for the drastically weakened parental position in modern American life. The children need a clear concept of what their privileges *and* responsibilities are in moral, sexual, and ethical matters.

The unique position of the Church, with the ability to speak to both sides of the parent–child axis, provides an excellent opportunity for exposition of moral values. The Church also is invested with authority and thus is unconsciously expected to define limits for all age groups.

Many parents of today are unsure of their own values and obviously cannot help communicating their indecision to their offspring. Laws or legislation regarding sexual behavior exist at the extremes of behavior: rape, incest, sexual offenses against minors, etc. The behavior discussed in this paper is not at these legal extremes in most people's view (although statutory rape *is* the issue many times). Thus the home, the law (and the schools), have declined or are unable to take a stand on the issue of sexual morality. If the Church also fails, it will have abandoned its position as an instrument of Christian education.

The Church's role as expositer of moral values is one that has long been assigned and accepted by its communicants. The authority exists for reinforcement of this role, and the Church must utilize the authority as well as assume its obligation. A clear, reasonable definition of what is morally acceptable in sexual behavior, as well as a clear statement of the moral, theological, and spiritual consequences of immorality, must be made. To do anything less will abrogate the Church's position and weaken its voice in the world. The clergy must lead the way, but the Department of Christian Education must also continue to reach the parishioners directly, especially young people, through its teaching process.

The issue is clear and the course of action is well defined. It only remains to act.

3

A SOCIOLOGY OF THE SEXUAL MORALITY OF YOUTH

SHORTLY after the appearance of a long article on sex morality in *Time* (January 24, 1964), several professors in a Louisiana university were discussing the problem. A philosophy professor summed it up this way:

> The typical American man wants women to be sexy and promiscuous—with the exception, that is, of his wife and his daughter.

These two exceptions—*my* wife and *my* daughter—and we could add "sister" as a third person whose morals we care about deeply—show the tension between hedonistic enjoyment and morality. The typical male wants women to be both good and bad. He wants his own wife to be true and faithful and his daughter to be popular while being sensible. With other men's wives and daughters and sisters, morality seems less important.

Very few men, no doubt, are free from temptation with respect to premarital and extramarital sex activity. Yet few (and many of the exceptions are confined to restrictive institutions) are totally amoral. Most of us feel guilty when we do wrong. We are more-or-less responsible members of the community. We do not want to hurt another person. We certainly do not want our wife or our daughter hurt. There does exist, then, a conflict of values in the culture itself, and thus in most of us. More of this later. We will focus here on youth and the problem of premarital sex behavior.

I. Statistical Problems on the Frequency of Sex Behavior

Accurate statistics giving the facts of sex relationships are not easy to come by. Most of the facts have been gathered by interviews between the individual and a scholarly researcher, which may lessen the extent of experiences reported. On the other hand, "bull sessions" may be characterized more by boasting and playful exaggeration than by precise reporting. We should, therefore, be careful of our "sampling." Sociologists report the adequacy of their samples; Johnny doesn't. This is not merely academic: when wild tales abound, many young people may be drawn aboard the bandwagon unconsciously and lower their own moral standards. Therefore, it will be valuable to review the studies showing frequencies of sex behavior. It is always valuable to know the truth; in the area of sex, to know it will probably decrease the bandwagon effect and will thus help preserve sound moral behavior based on rational choice, rather than fearful whim.

One further question of fact concerns the changing nature of sex practices.

II. How Fast Are Sex Practices Changing?

"Everybody knows that sexual immorality is much more widespread than it used to be." True or false? One hears it said by many individuals—by one's friends, by college professors, by clergymen. But is it true? Because this question is vital to our present understanding and action, let us go to the authority: Kinsey. (Incidentally, when Kinsey began publishing in 1948 many good statisticians questioned his data, especially, his sampling procedures. Today, however, this element of doubt has lessened. Kinsey's procedures and his data have withstood several detailed investigations and are held in higher esteem today than they were 20 years ago.

Chapter 11 of Kinsey's 1948 book on males is titled "Stability of Sexual Patterns"; it covers 54 pages and includes 42 tables and charts.[1] Kinsey (with his associates Pomeroy and Martin) starts by saying: "Many persons, of course, *believe* that patterns of sexual behavior have changed considerably in the last generation or two, (and they believe) that young people are sexually more precocious."[2] However, the scientist tests such propositions before accepting them, and Kinsey divided his male sample into two age groups, one averaging 22 years older than the other. "The older group represents the generation that was in its youth and, therefore, sexually most active from 1910 to 1925. These are the individuals who fought World War I and were responsible for the reputation of the 'roaring twenties.'"[3] The younger group was at the peak of its activity from the late 1920s to the years of World War II. Many comparisons were made between these two groups for three "educational class" levels (high, middle, and low) and for several types of sexual behavior. The details are fascinating, but over all, Kinsey concludes that sex practices did *not* change markedly over that period of time:

> Petting to climax shows a *slight* increase in frequency for all social levels. . . .[4]

> The younger generation appears to become active a year or two earlier . . . and this is true especially of men on the lowest educational levels.[5]

In general, the sexual patterns of the younger generation are so nearly identical with the sexual patterns of the older generation in regard to so many types of sexual activity that there seems to be no sound basis for the widespread opinion that the younger generation has become more active in its socio-sexual outlets.[6]

This is sobering testimony, coming from the only large-scale empirical study of comparative data gained over a period of time. Sex activity had increased, but only slightly and slowly. What about the generation since World War II? The magazines tell us that extramarital sex activity has zoomed "in recent years"; perhaps this is good business for the magazines. Our friends tell us the same thing. True or false?—this should be our question. A very sound conclusion would go something like this: "Mores change very slowly—this is a sociological axiom.[7] Sex mores changed slowly during the 'roaring twenties'—and they are still probably changing slowly today." Any speedup beyond this level *must be demonstrated empirically* before thinking men will believe it. True, men have continued to predict the onrushing tide of immorality, after Kinsey's clear findings. But they may be wrong, and the reader of this report will be wrong if he accepts such conclusions today without verification.

Kinsey's 1953 volume shows fairly similar results for women, although sex practices of women seem to have changed faster than those of men. The following table shows the proportion of young women, grouped by decade of birth, who had engaged in four types of sex activity by age 20.[8]

For each type of activity, the biggest shift came with the generation of women born during 1900–1909—those who were teenagers during World War I or "the roaring twenties." It is important to see that this significant shift

Sex Activity of Women by Age 20

	Women Born Before 1900	Women Born 1900–1909	Women Born 1910–1919	Women Born 1920–1929
Petted	66%	81%	90%	94%
Petted to Orgasm	10	17	22	28
Premarital Coitus	8	18	23	21
Coitus to Orgasm	4	8	11	11

did not continue at the same rate in later decades. The rate of increase actually slowed down since the decade of the 1920s, although a proportionate decrease appears only once. Kinsey: "The later generations appear to have accepted the new pattern and maintained or extended it." [9] And finally:

> This increase in the incidence of pre-marital coitus, and the similar increase in pre-marital petting, constitute the greatest changes which we have found between the patterns of sexual behavior in the older and younger generations of American females. (p. 298)

Although Kinsey's studies were concluded some 20 years ago, his research technique for assessing the ratio of change in sexual behavior is still valid. Thus the statement about the rapid increase in immorality in the last few years shows up in the light of Kinsey's empirically deduced conclusions as having some truth, much falsity.

From such data are we or are we not justified in caring further about the morality of youth today? This report is itself an index of our continuing concern. Our sex standards are changing, and in the direction of greater permissiveness. (An alternative way of getting an answer to whether or not immorality is on the rise is by studying the rates of illegitimacy and venereal disease—and these are rising.) What we need to learn, though, is that the common knowledge—the *gossip*—on this topic of immorality has been wrong before and quite possibly continues to be wrong today. We can disseminate this fact to check the bandwagon effect that *"everybody's* doing it, so why not me?"

Doing or Talking?

Talk about sex today is much more open, much more widespread than it was in earlier decades. Children talk about sex more and earlier today than formerly. Some parents are less afraid to discuss sex with their children (although they are still perhaps not frank enough with them).

The rules against discussing sex have certainly been relaxed. This is part of what *Time* meant in using the phrase "spectator sex"; sex is discussed and written about and pictured all around us. Let us be careful, however, and ask this question: "Just because we talk more about sex today, does this necessarily mean there is more extramarital or premarital sex activity?" To answer in the affirmative without investigation would be very careless. Everyone knows that many persons are big talkers, but that they seldom do many of the things they seem obsessed with verbally. *Talk* and *action* are two quite different things.

That there is more talk than action and that this is what we mean by a growing permissiveness would seem to be supported by the surveys in the sixties that show more significant change in attitude than we have found in behavior. For example, there would appear to be a movement among college men to reject, more and more, coitus without affection in favor of the same with affection, and for college women to become more permissive in regard to coitus with affection.[10] Ira Reiss would attribute this difference to a "consolidation process," in which attitude is now catching up with behavior.[11] Perhaps it could just as well represent a growing knowledge of the meaning of the person among our youth, of which there are some signs.

III. Published Data on Premarital Intercourse

"How much premarital intercourse is there?" This is, of course, a tough question, and even the experts disagree, but we will review the best existing knowledge on it. We will lean heavily on published empirical studies, which necessarily seem "old" when published because of the time and care required for good research to be done well. Let us remember that it has been established by the best authority that sex practices did not change rapidly during the first half of the twentieth century.

Time magazine's article quotes Dr. Graham B. Blaine, psychiatrist to the Harvard and Radcliffe Health Service, who estimates that "within the past 15 years the number of college boys who had intercourse before graduation rose from 50 per cent to 60 per cent, the number of college girls from 25 per cent to 40 per cent."

Here are several interesting notes on Dr. Blaine's figures: (1) they are estimates, not research data; (2) they are the highest estimates ever publicly given by a responsible authority; (3) they are made by a psychiatrist, and psychiatrists, as we know, tend to see more troubled people, less of a cross-section than the researchers do; (4) they are by an institutional psychiatrist, who may have chosen to "estimate" rather high for purposes of frightening authorities, parents, and students into some kind of counteraction, and (5) they are made about Harvard and Radcliffe students, long acknowledged as among the most sophisticated, modern undergraduates—pacesetters of style, perhaps—whose sex behavior is probably not outdone in many college circles.

With these relatively recent (1964) estimates in mind, and the precautions noted about them, let us proceed to the existing published data from empirical studies.

Kinsey found that the majority of persons who marry have had premarital sexual intercourse. The proportion for men is higher in the lower classes (98 per cent for men with grade school education; 85 per cent for those who attended some high school; 68 per cent among the group that had some college).[12]

Among the women interviewed in the 1940s, 49 per cent had sexual intercourse before marriage.[13] Most of this experience, however, was with the fiancé. This group includes from 45 to 70 per cent of all nonvirginal women.[14] More recent surveys among college people have corroborated these general findings. What is implied here is an unwritten cultural pattern: as a couple publicly demonstrates their greater affinity, becoming "pinned" and engaged, the community respects this growing commitment to marry by removing more and more chaperonage. Scores of other societies do the same thing with, of course, infinite variations. Thus, most of the nonvirgins at marriage have not been promiscuous (promiscuity involves relations with several persons); their sex activity has been with the husband-to-be. This is indeed a change, a new pattern, which probably has been coming on for half a century, with the increasing equality of the American female and her greater opportunities for college and job. Nobody has issued an engraved, stamped edict stating approval of the pattern, but it exists and must be faced.

We will examine these statistics more closely. Can we assume that 49 per cent of college-age girls have had sexual intercourse? The answer is no—due to a "class" factor. Girls from less privileged homes have had more of this kind of experience, and earlier. In 1963, Professor Winston Ehrmann, Florida sociologist, reviewed our knowledge about intercourse among college youth.

Many male undergraduates have had premarital intercourse, although the rate varies widely. It is as low as 32 per cent for a denominational college in Texas; it reaches 39 per cent in intermountain colleges, and it runs 51 per cent in the Midwest and goes as high as 73 per cent—but the last figure is for collegians who have had military service.[15] The rate appears to be increasing steadily, but again, not rapidly. Recent "open dormitory" practices in some colleges have spurred new rumors about immorality; these may or may not be well founded.

The rate is lower, of course, for college girls. The highest figure is 36 per cent for a northern college known for its liberal views. Other research finds rates of 28 per cent, 18 per cent, 14 per cent, and two colleges report 9 per cent each of premarital experience among their girls.[16] Smigel and Seiden in their very recent analysis of these and other surveys (1968) put the figure at an over-all 22 per cent for college women, which is very close to Kinsey's 20 per cent.

However, in a survey of college youth for his book *Sexual Wilderness*, published in 1968, Vance Packard found that the rate of coital behavior in college women had risen since Kinsey's survey to an over-all 43 per cent, whereas it had remained reasonably stable with college men at 58 per cent.[17] Although it is difficult to bring these figures into line with those of, say, Smigel and Seiden— and perhaps Packard's survey could be criticized on methodological grounds—it does coincide with two facts that we have already reported. First, that even with Kinsey it was noted that female sexual behavior is changing faster than male; and, second, that the change taking place seems to be a new demand for a love relationship for coitus among men and a new permissiveness of coitus with affection among women. It should be noted that the figures differ markedly when divided on a regional basis, and in the South, where the double standard still remains strong, the statistics support this contention.

This, briefly, represents the best available knowledge about the topic. The concerned adult can have confidence in these reports, and they can be found in any good college library. Ira Reiss, writing in *The New York Times* in 1967, concluded on the basis of such figures that "The sexual revolution [is] a myth and the only basic change [is] a trend toward more equality of the sexes. . . . There has been less change than [is] popularly believed between modern American males and their Victorian grandfathers." When, therefore, the young boy or girl states that "everyone's doing it," "it's the new thing," the priest, teacher, or parent can confidently challenge the youth to prove his assertions carefully on paper, listing specific instances of those who are known to indulge, those who are known not to, and all those about whom there is no information. You will find much less sure evidence than the youth originally supposed. You will find that he confuses petting with heavy petting, and heavy petting with intercourse, and that he leaps to conclusions about one couple from one glimpse, and from this couple to the entire group. You can refer him to published studies. And in the process, he will probably come to see more clearly the meaning of various actions—good and bad—for every human being. He should learn something about understanding, the

I–Thou relationship, human goodness and human weakness, sympathy, forgiveness, and justice in judging one's fellows. And he will see more clearly that there is another permitted road—the road of love, respect, and decency—while still grappling with the anxieties and promises of growing up.

IV. PETTING STATISTICS

There has been considerable increase in petting since World War I. Before that time, "sparking" and "spooning" occurred mostly between engaged couples. Today, as Professor Ehrmann puts it, "The typical youth, both male and female, dates from once to several times a week, and petting, more usually kissing although frequently more intimate fondling, occurs on a majority of these occasions. By the time of marriage, virtually all males and females have had petting experiences. . . ." [18] Again, these rates are higher for boys than for girls. How is this possible? It has been found that while many girls reject petting until they have known a boy for some time, there are a small number of girls who pet promiscuously with many boys. This is the way in which the rate differential is maintained between the average boy and girl.

The difference is shown in one of the findings from a study of 298 high school seniors in Louisiana in 1956. [19] One statement read: "I really have to like a person before I'll neck with him (or her)." Whereas 92 per cent of the girls agreed with the statement, only 47 per cent of the boys did. The girls clearly take existing moral standards more seriously than the boys do; perhaps we could add that they take *themselves* more seriously, too, when it comes to petting.

For women, the data for petting, and petting to climax are given above in the section dealing with rates of change.

This was one of the greatest changes in behavior found by Kinsey—petting to orgasm among women.

It is important to observe here that these statistics, as well as those of the previous section, have received considerable support from a study (1964) reported by Mervin Freedman that is valuable because of its relative recency and its methodological rigor.[20] It reports a careful sampling of undergraduate girls at an eastern women's college, within the 5 years preceding the study. Forty-nine girls were interviewed several times a year during their four years of college, and their responses were checked by questionnaires given several hundred of their classmates. Briefly, it found that as of the senior year, 6 per cent had shown "uninhibited behavior" (promiscuous intercourse), 16 per cent had engaged in intercourse "confined to serious relationships," 41 per cent had experienced "extensive petting," 27 per cent "restricted petting," and 10 per cent "limited experience." Of special interest is the observation among the 16 per cent that few said they had guilt about intercourse with the man they loved, but rather found it a rewarding experience. Little guilt feeling was found, in fact, among any of the girls.

Freedman's report concluded:

> It is likely that promiscuity occurs more frequently among high school girls than among college women. . . . There is no evidence, from the MMPI [a personality test] for example, that either relative sexual freedom or abstinence are associated with signs of neurosis. . . . Despite an appearance of worldliness and sophistication, it seems that conservatism, inhibition of impulse, cautiousness, and willingness to defer gratification are part and parcel of American middle-class character.[21]

These findings reject the prediction of Terman in 1938 that the female unmarried virgin would disappear by 1960, and Binger's 1961 comment that "The contemporary mores of young people are so different from those which governed their parents' or teachers' lives that a common meeting ground between them scarcely exists. . . ." Finally, we report that these findings are very similar to findings we recently made in a large state university and a large private university.

V. Who or What Has Caused the Change?

From the foregoing, it seems clear that at least the *apparent* morality of the Victorian period is receding. Why is this? What causes it? Who is to blame? To take the last question, obviously no particular person or group can be blamed. Not that many persons don't try to fix the blame. Sometimes we blame the bomb or the automobile, industrialization or the city, parents or the kids themselves. All of these doubtless play a part.

Many blame the mass media of communication—movies, magazines, television, newspaper stories, etc.[22] On this point, some strong counterarguments can be made. In the first century, Martial blamed loose morals on horse racing and gladiatorial combats. In the sixteenth century, moralizers were blaming the troubadors. In eighteenth-century England, cheap novels were held to be the ruination of moral codes. Flaubert, a century ago, pointed scornfully at the vulgar periodicals flowing out of Paris. Then it was the Sunday supplements, movies, radio, and television. However, since the Payne Foundation study of movies and children in the 1930s, not a single scholarly study of the impact of the media has supported these rather easy claims.[23] Certainly, some individuals may intensify their baser nature by being exposed to mass-media communication, but it helps not at all to be content with this approach.

On the other hand, one can argue that television, for example, is a supreme upholder of the Golden Rule! Watch TV sometime from this point of view and see for yourself. (None of this is to say that we should abandon our efforts to correct the abuses of the media; we should continue to write broadcasters and publishers, demanding improved programing.)

Should we blame the parents? Of course, when they fail, by word and deed, to help their children understand the Christian way of life. Parents are the first and most vital influence on children. But a whole psychology of child-raising is implied in this one sentence, and we need not expand it here. We may as well blame the schools, Darwin, Freud, and—yes, the churches! Our concern should not be to condemn the twentieth century, but to understand it and attempt to deal with it by seeking the values we believe in by the most effective means at hand.

The cause, then, of changing sex standards is the entire transformation of civilization in our time.[24] Are these standards wholly sinful and wrong? Recall the findings of premarital intercourse among college woman—roughly one in four girls has experienced intercourse. (However, almost every college girl in the stories and movies just happens to look like the fourth one!) What about the other three in this quartet? What this tells us about American civilization today is that we have not just one set of standards, but several. And perhaps this can tell us a great deal about the predicament of the individual youth. He or she is uncertain, concerned, anxious, troubled, not positive about what kind of a self to build. There is, then, a conflict of values among us. Today most of us still face the dilemma of deciding, "What am I to do?" It is both an individual conflict—you and I have both felt it—but it is also a collective conflict and has been since the dawn of time.

What is the Christian attitude? This question is dealt with in other sections of this report. Is it clear, consistent, logical, unimpeachable? Is it workable within the context of the lives of youth in the 1970s? Can youth accept it as we do? We as Christian spokesmen must be able to discuss these issues in love, honesty, and dignity with our boys and girls. The youngster can be prepared to make a choice that will affect his entire life, that he must be willing to follow, and for which he knows he must accept the consequences. If youth are aided in forming this philosophy, they are more likely to make a mature choice with respect to sex behavior, and they will become adult individuals prepared to solve the many equally important problems facing them.

Perhaps we can state one typical goal for our times. It should not center around threadbare materialism, but should be the goal of a strong, happy family, composed of husband, wife, and children who love and respect each other, God, and their fellowman, and who are playing their part in a healthy community life.

This is a great deal. Is it too much to ask? Many of us will fail in the achievement of it, but the attempt is something we owe ourselves and we should not shirk the effort. We owe it to our parents and others, too, but when we pledge the effort to ourselves, we gain integrity, we become whole. There is an axiom, implicit in most sociology and social psychology, to the effect that all humans desire self-respect and through this, the respect of others. The Don Juan fails in this—both in his own heart and in the judgment of others.

With respect to this ideal goal, the churchman can take a good look at his own parish. How much success or failure does he see around him on these grounds? How many actually face up to it? How many would rather ignore it? It can be most embarrassing! And how many parishioners measure up to this goal? What might the churchman now start to do to contribute his part to constructing a different picture?

VI. Danger Points and Some Discussion

Where are the danger points for youth? Sociological studies focus on several situations here, but one of these seems paramount. This is the situation of "going steady." It has been found that heavy petting tends not to occur on the first date, or in random dating, at least among the overwhelming majority of cases, especially where the girl has self-respect.[25] When, however, John and Jane have gone out together for weeks or months, the pressure starts to build. They spend many hours alone together, typically after an evening of study, or after a show or a dance. John, with his greater sex drive, plus his view of masculinity and his need to prove his virility in the face of possible fears of homosexuality, is often interested in further sex experimentation, greater intimacy. Jane, less biologically impelled, wishes to show her affection. She does not want to lose John. Thus both are willing to pet, and often do. What will be the outcome? Will Jane become the "fourth girl"?

Here we have the crux of the problem in every community and every school. John has normal masculine drives —he is a human male. He also "knows" some of his friends are "getting their kicks." (He probably does not know exactly who, or in what form, but complete information and rational, light-of-day behavior is not optimal in the situation.) At the extreme, he may let Jane know that if she refuses to submit, he will drop her. At this point, Jane may drop him, and accept dates with other boys. Or, as is often the case, she may wish to continue the relationship. All girls want dates, especially with "nice boys like John."

The fear of being excluded from parties is a real one for her, and we must never forget or minimize this. John and Jane keep dating, and there are more hours in the car after the show. Liquor obviously can play a significant role here. What does Jane do? Clearly, John and Jane need to know the possible consequences of their actions.

These consequences are all too well known: abortion, illegitimacy, school dropouts (which result in the girl falling behind her husband's cultural attainment, as well as in the boy's tragic failure to achieve his proper level of vocation), divorce itself (the proportion of divorces from teenage marriages is exceedingly high),[26] and often a 50 per cent lower income potential. There is, above all, the tragic inner hurt to all concerned persons: the parents as well as the boy and girl, but especially the girl, who can suffer the most and may never fully recover.

All counselors are familiar with this typical situation. Certainly most boys and girls are, too, but they might not see it with clarity. It is certainly our responsibility to help them.

Certain sociological principles can provide some light at this point. One is that the girl has the power to flash either the green light or the red. This is not a surprising statement, and it has significance. The Louisiana study of high school seniors made the following test:[27] the boys and girls were asked to agree or disagree with two statements. The first was: "If the girl says 'no' and the boy does not think she means it, he should stop." Forty-one per cent of the boys and 61 per cent of the girls agreed. Next they were given this statement: "If the girl says 'no' and the boy thinks she means it, he should stop." To this statement, 96 per cent of the girls and 89 per cent of the boys agreed.

This single finding—and it has since been corroborated in other studies—[28] demonstrates that there is a clear norm among youth that the girl is expected to set the limits and that the boy should respect the wishes and standards of the girl. The rule that "one should not entice a good girl" still seems to be part of teenage culture. This form of "chivalry" is not dead. Sociologist David Riesman was quoted in *Time* as saying that boys treat girls as *persons*, rather than as *objects*, far more today than in the 1920s. The girl can say "no," but responsibility is shared by the boy; he should respect the wishes and values of the girl, as well as his own better nature. He has something to lose, too—his honor, as judged by his own conscience.

The second sociological principle about morality among youth deals with groups. Where do youth get their sex standards? We would like to answer this by saying "from parents, from church." But we know that a vital source of values comes from the peer group. Most boys and girls will do as their friends are doing. (So will most adults, for that matter!) Knowing this, however, gives us some leverage to work with. If we can help our children to develop mature standards of judgment about people, then we can have more confidence in their individual behavior. St. Paul says in I Corinthians 15:33, "Bad company ruins good morals." Of course, many old chestnuts point up the same conclusion: "Birds of a feather flock together" and "A man is known by his friends" and "One bad apple spoils the whole barrel," and so on. Just exactly how to provide this healthy group atmosphere is discussed elsewhere in this report.

There is perhaps a third principle. Some studies have shown that youth, in their anxiety and uncertainty, want guidance and counsel from understanding elders. They are "adrift in a sea of permissiveness," as *Time* puts it. Maybe they will not admit it. Maybe they will appear to ignore it. However, there are many examples of gratitude for controls imposed from above. In one eastern college, girls privately told counselors that they were grateful for the curfew recently imposed on them. And one reason they gave was "that extra hour parked with John can be awfully trying." Another situation is the party. Are all teenagers against supervision by parents? Probably not. The social disorganization of our times is characterized by anomie, the absence of clear standards. The more alert of our youth know this. We can help to acquaint them with the authentic standards; we should do so, and many youth secretly will be glad to have us do so.

Finally, we can interpret youth to themselves. They are so caught up in being alive that they do not stop to observe themselves. We can show them goals, we can show them standards, and we can show them how their groups work. For example, we can talk to them about the pressure put on girls by boys, and on boys by other boys. We can tell them about the superficiality of their popularity criteria: the short-term run of athletic success for boys; and being "a good date" for girls. Adolescence in America has often been seen as a time of responsibility;[29] we can remind them that in a few short years they will be out of school, starting a family, and being evaluated by standards of adulthood. This will not reach many youth immediately—they will not want to hear these things. But coupled with some basic discussion of ethics and individual growth, this is a time to try to reach as many as possible with a philosophy of life that will be their best preparation for adulthood.

Undoubtedly, what we have said here implies a spirit of communication between adults and youth, and it may occur to the reader that this is the very thing that our society seems to lack. We are all familiar with the rather tired saying, "Don't trust anyone over thirty." Certainly there has always been a segment of our youth with which realistic communication is difficult. This group is all the more obvious today. How large it may be is debatable. If identified with the so-called young radicals of the college campus, the estimate runs between 2 and 5 per cent. The proportion undoubtedly grows as we speak of older groups. Yet even among these young people—adolescents and young adults—it would be a mistake to write them off as simply promiscuous and not susceptible to dialogue—if we really mean *dialogue*. Radical youth often possess a very strong sexual code, much more thought out than that of our conformist youth, and it is based upon a deep personalism not unlike what we advocate in this study.[30] This is not to say, however, that the "generation gap" is not often used as an excuse for sexual patterns that would be better described as pathological.

However, aside from our more radical youth, the vast majority of young people present us with the same unimaginative "frat house" sexuality, which probably reflects our unwillingness to engage the hard questions of value more than it reflects their determination not to listen.[31] It is not enough merely to tell John and Jane about the dangers of pregnancy and suddenly terminated school careers, the horrors of abortion, and the heartaches over guilt and shame. They must also get a set of positive standards, Christian values that have endured for centuries. These values are the same as those that apply to all other social relationships, but on this question they can be located directly within the framework of marriage, parenthood, work, and community. Sex education is not a course in biology; it is encompassed by the ideals of raising boys and girls in a frank, honest, loving Christian community.

* 4 *

MASS COMMUNICATION
MEDIA AND MORALITY

DURING the 1950s parents complained to the television networks that "trashy junk about space flights" was being broadcast. Such gripes came to an abrupt halt on October 4, 1957, with Sputnik I. A minor issue, but somewhat characteristic of the criticism of mass-media communication in general. The media are a convenient target for abuse or, at least, an easy scapegoat for all kinds of behavior and attitudes, including the charge that the media promote promiscuity. A great wave of guilt swept the industry following the tragic assassination of Robert Kennedy, and there was the promise of relatively violence-free television. Yet, in the cold light of examined viewer ratings and apparent fondness for murder and mayhem, most programs remain the same as before.

What we must do is take a hard look at the assumption that television and other forms of the communication media do affect our moral character. Is this true or false? To answer this question, we will search the literature in two areas: (1) the *content* of the media, with respect to sex standards, and (2) what little is known about the *effects* of this content on youth.

I. MEDIA CONTENT

Much has been done in content analysis of the media. Here are some of the findings:

Saenger analyzed 156 comic strips in the press.[1] "In keeping with middle-class morality, there were practically no divorced or separated men and women." Elkin analyzed old western movies, now frequently seen on TV.[2] Justice, he found, always prevailed. The typical hero neither smoked nor drank, did not lose his temper, fought fair, and was a paragon of democratic social attitudes. (This "Galahad," it is true, has been to some extent replaced by the "adult cowboy" of recent years, but he still epitomizes many traditional values of our society.)

Arnheim's study of radio soap operas concluded that "poetic justice always obtains."[3] W. Lloyd Warner, the anthropologist of "Yankee City," interviewed many women about their relationship to the soap opera "Big Sister."[4] Ruth, the heroine, attacked problems through the exercise of honesty, patience, and moral rectitude, going to the extent of rejecting any exercise of sexual impulse! And still another of the classic studies by Herzog found city women telling the interviewer, "You can learn refinement from Our Gal Sunday."[5] Studies at Newcomb College have drawn such conclusions about the family TV dramas as: "The family is good—it must be preserved"; "children are good to have, whether they are sometimes troublesome or not"; "even homely girls have a chance at marriage, and beautiful girls have love problems too"; "fair play is extolled"; "the 12 Boy Scout laws well summarize the morals of TV dramas"; "consideration for and civility toward others is frequently shown as a good thing"; etc.[6] Surely, "Father Knows Best" of a decade ago was only the forerunner of a whole string of situation comedies, usually utterly inane, that have followed in recent years and have won great acclaim from PTAs, education groups, and other organizations of concerned adults. Programs such as "That Woman," "The Mothers-in-Law," and "Occasional Wife" (a very antisexual and consequently bad show) come to mind.

The editor and critic, Norman Podhoretz, watched the family dramas as they emerged as a new, show-business type in the early 1950s, and he believed he found a new hero—the American father (in contrast to the Jiggs-Dagwood buffoon).[7] "The great reality of his life, the sphere in which things happen to him, is the family. . . . We find him telling his daughter that marriage, children and love are far more important than fame or wealth. . . . He represents reasonableness, tolerance and good will . . . the image of American maturity."

This review of empirical studies will surprise many. Some parents express horror at the media; they consider them pornography at its worst. These parents are correct if they are referring to a few comic books; magazines for the "sophisticated young male," such as *Playboy* (although one might question whether the unreal object depicted in their centerfold and elsewhere is capable of evoking an erotic reaction); the explicit novel, such as John Updike's *Couples* or Philip Roth's *Portnoy's Complaint*; and in particular the growing number of sexually oriented movies coming out of Hollywood and elsewhere.

A word needs to be said about attempts at self-regulation among some of these media. In the 1950s, in response to public and governmental criticism, the comic book publishers agreed to apply some standards to what they distributed. Long prior to this, in the 1920s, Hollywood had issued its famous production code, enforced by the so-called Hayes Office. The codes of radio and television followed suit. When the older Hollywood code seemed no longer to meet the prevailing standards of the movie-going public—who now demand something closer to what is seen on the stage—this code was revised. The 1968 revision of the Production Code of the Motion Picture Association of America gives one of four ratings to a film, and leaves it up to the viewer to make his decision. The ratings are:

$X =$ No one under 17 admitted.
$R =$ Persons under 17 admitted only with a parent or guardian.
$GP =$ Suggested for mature audiences.
$G =$ Suggested for general audiences.

While enforcement of this code depends somewhat on the local theater operator (we note, for example, some places where the age limit is raised to 18) and ultimately on the public, there are indications that it results in some economic sanctions and consequently improves the quality of the films produced.[8]

Of course, this is simply a way of policing the fact that the American consumer demands more sexually explicit material in his movie entertainment. In the 1960s, such subjects as homosexuality (*The Killing of Sister George*; *The Fox*; *Staircase*), masturbation (*The Fox*; *The Silence*; *The Girl on the Motorcycle*—before cutting), adultery (*The Graduate*; *Julia*), and fornication (*Three in an Attic*, which was really more a very tired "dirty joke" than anything else) were treated widely. By the end of the decade, scenes of coitus on the movie screen were fairly commonplace. Whether all or any of these are considered pornographic is a question that not even the United States Supreme Court finds easy to answer; and undoubtedly much depends on one's age, emotional stability, education, and values (which inevitably differ from person to person in a pluralistic society). Of course, there will always be a "black market" in pornography, such as the sending of filthy pictures through the mails. There will always be the use of sex for the purposes of advertising products unrelated to our erotic needs—and this is perhaps the most devastating form of obscenity.

But on the whole, we would still insist that the media are not only unpornographic, but are, in fact, often exceedingly and extremely unimaginatively moral. Even a recent book, *The Pious Pornographers*, shows that while the women's magazines are printing discussions of sex in great detail, they do so in a serious, protoscientific way. Sociologists have long followed the generalization: Media reinforce values. This is a statement about "effects," which we come to next; but surely the burden of content research shows that these images disseminated via the media are not sexy and immoral, but rather reflect the picture of America as it would like to be.

Nothing said here implies that we are satisfied with the media performance. Few clergy or educators doubt that the media could produce much better fare. They could be a mass education force of tremendous impact. They could bring to the millions a feeling for modern times; for social change; for new developments, which with more support would better mankind in numerous ways; for greater appreciation of the complexity and the promise of the world. Some programs and articles (and the BBC "Third Programme") accomplish this. Most, of course, are stereotyped and patterned. Most show Man as a one- or two-dimensional being. Our point, however, is much more modest: we are saying that the media do not encourage illicit sexual behavior to the extent that we sometimes—in moments of panic—think they do.

II. DATA ON THE EFFECTS OF MEDIA

We do not, in fact, know very much about the direct impact of the media on sex behavior. Only recently in a study of this question S. H. Lovibond wrote: "Despite the social importance of this question, there is little scientifically acceptable evidence on which the issue can be decided." [9] We will attempt to report those studies that bear indirectly on the topic, as well as the few that attempt some tentative answer.

Everybody blames the media for something. This turns out to be either personal opinion or reports of one particular individual who is said to have violated a norm because of exposure to a certain media presentation. For example, the assassin of President McKinley was reported to have had in his pocket a copy of a Hearst newspaper excoriating the President. More recently the chief critic of the media for their harmful effects on youth was the New York psychiatrist, Frederick Wertham.[10] His argument typically involves particular youths who are said to have committed crimes and bizarre acts following their exposure to a given film or comic book. It is equally germane to ask about the youths' families or their relationship to society generally.

Much more recently than Wertham, Harry J. Skornia argues that there is bountiful evidence—"from several hundred correctional institutions, hospitals, schools, juvenile courts, psychiatric clinics, and mental hospitals around the world"—that television is one of the most powerful dimensions of a person's environment, constantly teaching him all kinds of antisocial behavior.[11] Aside from the sources he cites, Skornia depends heavily for his conclusions upon the Payne Foundation study of movies and children (noted on page 50). It is clear that in stating his position—which he does almost hysterically—Skornia is drawing upon a psychological model rather than a sociological method. For example, he criticizes surveys that disagree with him because they ask children for responses, instead of asking those who work with children, observe their behavior, and look for its unconscious causes.[12] It is also worth noting that Skornia depends particularly upon professionals who work with deviant children, and thus he creates a bias similar to that created by psychiatrists judging the existence of a sexual revolution (referred to on page 44). Yet he insists, not without power of conviction, that the values in television are essentially destructive of our society, and that they effect in a substantial manner the thinking of our youth.[13]

It is difficult to know what to make of this position of Wertham and Skornia from a sociological point of view. As we shall see, there is reason to believe there is an element of truth in their claims. However, we shall present more representative data on this topic—for example, Lovibond's rather excellent study from Adelaide, Australia—that will put things in better perspective.

In analyzing the effects of the media, contemporary social science abandons the older assumption that media act like hypodermic needles; the program or editorial "triggers" the individual—as Skornia still suggests[14]—into a stimulus–response act without any involvement or mediation of daily life. Today we tend to see the media as one more facet of daily life, one stimulus among many, which is not atomized within us, but which serves as a basis for our social conversation, for our orientation to particular issues, and in many ways forms part of the environment within which we act. Many individual studies since about 1940 have contributed to this theory. They have been analyzed and summarized best by Joseph Klapper over a period of some 15 years. His book is the basic one for our purposes.[15] Interestingly enough, while it was published only five years before Skornia's study and is the only book-length examination of the problem, the Skornia study never mentions Klapper's work. Kyle Haselden's lucid little book *Morality and the Mass Media*, published three years after Skornia's, depends heavily on Klapper.[16]

A study of the radio-listening habits of 3,125 elementary

and junior high school children in Connecticut revealed no difference in nervous habits, fears, daydreams, and frustration reactions between those who did and those who did not listen to crime, anticrime, and adventure stories.[17] A later study of 260 12- and 13-year-old boys in New York City yielded similar results.[18] The monumental study in Britain by Himmelweit, Oppenheim, and Vince found likewise: "no more aggressive, maladjusted, or delinquent behavior among viewers than among non-viewers." [19] This British study reports detailed findings from four communities involving several thousand children. One part of the study was able to compare children in two cities of great similarity, only one of which had TV reception. In New York, Wolf and Fiske, using comic books as the medium, also found little evidence of distasteful consequences, although some neurotic children tended to use media heroes as stimuli to aggressive or escapist fantasy.[20]

The Lovibond study, to which we have already referred, was like the Himmelweit, Oppenheim, and Vince research in that it was able, over a two-year period, to compare children who had not been exposed to television and those who had (since television came to Adelaide during that period). As a result of his work Lovibond makes the following statement, which would appear an unqualified endorsement of those who, like Wertham and Skornia, point out the great teaching power of media:

> The two studies [two years apart] would appear to have established quite firmly that there is a relationship between exposure to crime and violence media and endorsement of an ideology which makes the use of force in the interest of ego-centric needs the essential content of human relationships.[21]

But he makes a qualification of this bald statement, which brings it more into line with what Klapper, the British research, Wolf and Fiske, and (as we shall see) others say. It is that *no one-cause relationship can be established*, and that we must take into account "temperamental characteristics which predispose some children" to negative influence from television. In other words, television can be a reinforcement of a taste for violence, but we cannot say that it is the cause.[22] This, of course, is no reason to praise television.

Three other recent studies give some support to facets of this general thesis. Walter Gerson, in examining the effect of mass media in the process of socialization of black men as compared to white, notes that the former are more readily influenced than the latter because they are predisposed to adopt white ways as necessary for success in our WASP society.[23] Haddon Robinson, in studying the impact of religious radio and television, tells us that he finds such programs effective educational tools principally where people are already Christians and hence predisposed to what they hear or see.[24] In another article exploring the ability of broadcasting to influence sanitation procedures in some of the more primitive parts of the world, the author discovered that change was all the more marked when the information offered was in minimal conflict with traditional attitudes and prejudices.[25]

This kind of data is what prompts Klapper to suggest that the causal sequence may work in the other direction: "the existing psychological orientation of audience members determines their reactions to violent media fare." That the psychological disposition comes before the viewing in time is contained in Maccoby's 1954 report, showing that children in homes with much tension, physical punishment, and distant mother–child relationships spend a greater amount of time in front of TV than children in more permissive homes.[26]

One wonders to what extent this situation was operative in the very interesting findings in 1964 of Richard Nakewicz and Stanley Graven, reported to the American Academy of Pediatrics. These two medical doctors found television operating in a most "McLuhanesque" fashion. It was not necessarily the content of the program but the involvement of the child watching the media from three to ten hours a day, every day, that resulted in nervousness, continuous fatigue, headaches, loss of sleep, bellyaches, and sometimes vomiting, which they called "the tired child syndrome." [27] Something is happening here, but is it happening to our values?

Other findings in the British study of Himmelweit *et al.*, to which we referred before, are relevant, although indirect. "Contrary to expectation, television did not make children more interested in appearance or in fame and glamour. But it did make them (especially the adolescent boys) more interested in the things they would like to own, such as cars and houses, than in the work they would like to do." Viewers showed "a more realistic or adult awareness of the prestige attaching to various jobs." Television viewers were more ambitious about jobs. TV had no effect on increasing desire for a "glamorous" job. Girl viewers, asked about expectations related to marriage and choice of mate, mentioned such qualities as kindness and lack of jealousy more often than did nonviewers. Controls (nonviewers), more so than viewers, wanted husbands to be "good providers" and to "take them out."

Much has been said about whether television is "good" or "bad" for children. How do we answer this question? The above data from the British study can be interpreted according to one's own standards. British television fans were reported, again, as doing slightly less well in school work, but doing more chores around the home. Never did the TV viewers show up as clearly inferior to the non-viewers. Librarians often say children ask for books dealing with a program they have seen; others say TV keeps children away from more rewarding activities.

We know something about this from two large-scale surveys of adults in the United States. A 1961 Gallup poll showed that 8 per cent of a national sample protested the "immorality and sex" of television in its impact on children; in the same study, 16 per cent protested the intransigence of newspapers and 28 per cent objected to excessive violence on television.[28] In a 1960 study of 2,498 adults, only about a fifth of the respondents could think of an actual example where some child they knew had been harmed or had done something harmful as a result of television.[29] Almost a third could mention something good that resulted for a particular child. Most (about two-thirds) agreed that children were better off with than without television.

Most relevant to our topic, only 5 per cent of the sample picked the category "sex, suggestiveness, vulgarity" as a main disadvantage of TV. On the other hand, violence drew 33 per cent, and 37 per cent felt that television kept children from homework, chores, bed, etc."

We must ask, finally: How relevant is television to teenagers? Interviews by Social Research, Inc., of Chicago suggest that teenagers may have special stars as their favorites, but they tend to feel that television is mostly for children and for established families, and they do not watch it very much.

It must also be noted that all of this varies with the age of the child, the kinds of programs watched, who is present when watching, the existing character or personality of the child, and certainly his family situation, now and earlier. Certainly all kinds of effects result from television. It remains to be demonstrated that these are overwhelmingly bad, or overwhelmingly good.

III. DISCUSSION

We have seen that the content of the media (especially television, which has been the subject of the most recent research), is much more conventional than it is pornographic. To quote one more study: "The average pattern of personality stereotype of all heroes was found to correspond closely with the values held by our culture, while that for villains was generally antithetical to those values." [30] Most of the time, the media reinforce the values of the society; this is quite clear. In fact, this can be part of its very problem. In a society which feels comfortable only in the presence of the banal, the program that challenges our superficial suppositions and goads our consciences is not destined for a long run. Anxiety is a necessary concomitant for change—at least so we would argue[31]—and change we certainly need. "Bonanza" occasionally has raised some social issues in its endless recountings of the all-American Cartwright family; but not to any noticeable degree. "The Smothers Brothers" program made its point without a doubt, and perhaps sometimes with a rather heavy hand; its fate in the spring of 1969 is common knowledge.

We have seen from published studies that the *effects* of the media fail to show the primary or principal cause of moral deterioration in children. Rather, while there are many effects, television fans show rather slight differences from nontelevision fans. (Typically, our studies utilized a "control" technique, comparing heavy consumers with lighter consumers.) How valid are these studies? These data, gathered and interpreted by social scientists (who are inclined to be "intellectual" and rather unfavorable to the mass media), are, one could hardly argue, biased in *favor* of the media. Perhaps, although social scientists are basically critical, they are not as antimedia as literary critics.

Furthermore, the conclusions of the social scientists are shared to a large extent by the learning theorists. Understandably, in our times the teaching of values and morals has become a subject for examination. The consensus is that the family is the fundamental source of such learning, since a moral sense is derived from identifications made by the individual in the context of his most immediate relationships (parents and siblings, then teachers and peers). As Louis Raths *et al.*, tell us in *Values and Teaching*, it is when the family breaks down (as it all too frequently does, with tragic consequences) that the individual is presented with no guidance in the many value options presented him by communication and travel.[32] It is then that he becomes susceptible to the more "visceral suggestions" of television, the movies, and literature. But this kind of "acting out" (irresponsible behavior indicative of a weak identity structure) should not be confused with the young person's *reasoned moral decision* that happens to be in disagreement with our own. Tolerance and flexibility, as moral qualities, are closely related to family stability and intimacy, as Barry Sugarman has pointed out.[33] Kenneth Keniston, in *The Young Radicals*, carefully documents the fact that youth who protest the Vietnam War are *not* sociopathic victims of the allurements of television (brainwashing). They are the predictable products of highly moral homes.[34]

Not everyone will be satisfied that this report is valid. Many readers will remember a particular disagreeable incident and blame the media for it. The report does accurately reflect empirical research, however; our opinion about the performance of the media is a different matter. We have already said that we could envision a far finer job of programming than we are now getting.

The question remains: How is this to be attained? Should we demand censorship of the media? We think not.

Martial in Rome

This has been tried for ages against the classics and the media and, indeed, against the Bible and some of its Old Testament stories involving sex. Censorship is basically immoral. The late Kyle Haselden, who was deeply committed at great price to both social and private morality, wrote: "Freedom is always primary and privileged. Censorship should always be suspect." [35] He would allow censorship of only those media that are readily available to children (e.g., television), and then only in a very limited an occasional notable exception), but in a strange form. Human sexual behavior, which is not in any sense against the law within marital bonds, is absolutely forbidden; but murder, theft, assault and other forms of violence, all decidedly illegal, are depicted daily.

Since censorship is not really the answer, what can we do? We can exert pressure on the media producers at points where we dislike a particular product. We can also encourage them to strengthen the quality of their fare, to raise their sights. It is said that when NBC receives one letter from a fan, they read it; and when they get two, they call a major staff conference. We can influence them almost as much as they influence us.

* 5 *

MASTURBATION

THIRTY years ago one would have thought long and hard before even broaching the subject of masturbation in a church-sponsored publication. Condemned by everyone from medical doctors to the Boy Scout manual, there was little to discuss about it. Now we have more understanding of this phenomenon, and while there appears to be no clear unanimity in the mind of the Church, we would undoubtedly be shirking our responsibility if we did not consider the subject in a study such as this and advance our own conviction.

By masturbation we mean what Masters and Johnson call "automanipulation." [1] This is the stimulation of one's own genitals by whatever means one may conceive (Masters and Johnson describe a number of means in a scientific manner with what amounts to a comic effect). Sometimes we speak of "mutual masturbation," which refers to two people, either heterosexual or homosexual, stimulating to orgasm one or both partners. Hettlinger seems to indicate that in the case of so-called heterosexual mutual masturbation, the term "masturbation" is a misnomer, and he would have us speak of "petting to climax." [2] (I agree wholeheartedly with what he has to say on this subject and refer those interested to his book.) Homosexual mutual masturbation is another question, which would be more profitably discussed under the question of homosexuality in general, and does not lie within the scope of this work.

When we speak of masturbation, or automanipulation, it is important to think of it as practiced by three different

age groups: children from approximately three to six
(infantile masturbation), adolescents, and adults. Infantile
masturbation is virtually universal, instinctual, and devoid
of moral content. We shall not discuss it any further here.
Adolescent masturbation is the usual area of concern, and
our comments shall be directed principally to this phenomenon, with some reference to its adult development.

The question is not whether boys will masturbate. According to Kinsey 92 per cent do.[3] Generally, the onset of
this kind of activity is at about age 13 or 14, although it
can occur as early as 9 or 10 or as late as 16 to 18 years.[4]
The question is: What moral judgments do we make upon
masturbation? There is no doubt about the official position
of the Roman Catholic Church, which condemns the practice as a mortal sin.[5] It would be difficult to mount opposition to the papal position simply on the grounds of the
near-universal practice of masturbation; pride is even more
widely prevalent, and we are not about to declare that
sinless. But, as we shall see, there is testimony by many
psychiatrists and clergy as to the positive value of masturbation, and it is therefore not at all surprising to discover
some ambivalence in the mind of the Church, at least, as to
the moral status of masturbation.

Known for his vigorous condemnation of this activity
is the renowned and widely respected Anglican theologian,
the Rt. Rev. R. C. Mortimer. Bishop Mortimer writes:

Those who practise this vice . . . grow soft. They lose
resolution, courage, and initiative. They lose mental vigour
and alertness. Their lives become centred on trivialities,
their thirst for pleasure and excitement grows, they become
selfish, luxurious, and unable to bear discomfort or to overcome difficulties. And when the time for marriage comes
they are unprepared and unable to bear its responsibilities or
to abide by its loyalties. They are unfit for adult life. The

prime root cause of this softness lies in the selfish pursuit of pleasure for its own sake.[6]

At least he did not say that excessive masturbation drives you insane; which, Masters and Johnson discovered, was the common opinion in the male study group of which they inquired.[7] But it is rather incredible in the face of 92 per cent participation that Mortimer is ready to label such people as "unprepared for marriage," "centred on trivialities," and "unfit for adult life."

The bishop—who, it must be said, is neither purgatorial nor joyless by nature—considers masturbation "another form of perversion" like contraception.[8] He believes any voluntary ejaculation (since he does not mention nocturnal emissions we will assume he permits involuntary ejaculations) that does not intend to allow the possibility of conception is sinful; it is the unwarranted use of our sexual capacity for the purpose of pleasure only. He is thoroughly consistent in this position, outdoing the Roman Catholic Church and condemning even the rhythm method and (incredible as it may seem) coitus during pregnancy.[9] He does not mention coitus after menopause, but it would seem to follow that this is sinful also because, while acknowledging the "unitive aspect of marriage," he is clearly unhappy with coitus as anything but primarily for the means of reproduction.[10]

The fact that Bishop Mortimer is willing to pursue the logic of his position to its bitter end reveals to us in unmistakable terms the major premise of his position. It is the same premise that, as we shall see, characterizes Roman Catholic teaching; what Hettlinger calls a "superstitious reverence for semen." [11] Somehow male semen is conceived of as almost possessing human life by itself, and its wastage as little short of murder. This is a highly untenable position, since any normal ejaculation is likely to contain several hundred million sperm, all of which will be "wasted" inevitably save perhaps one or, on very rare occasions, two. Biologically it is unsound, since the female ovum is also needed to produce human life. Yet how else can one interpret Mortimer's fear of voluntary ejaculation when there is no possibility of union with the female ovum?

There is certainty behind the Roman Catholic statement, promulgated by Pius XII; namely, that masturbation is not permitted even to obtain semen for medical purposes, such as fertility counts and artificial insemination. If a doctor is to assist in the insemination of the wife by the husband (the use of a donor is obviously forbidden), he can do so only after the husband has ejaculated within the vagina of the wife.[12] Further indication that in Roman Catholic thinking the sinfulness of masturbation centers in the wastage of semen is, as Glanville Williams points out, that female masturbation (with no ejaculation) is not always considered sinful and is in fact permitted under certain circumstances. This would be when the husband has achieved orgasm without the wife having done so, thus not having satisfied her needs, or if the wife wishes to make coitus easier for herself.[13] The concession is certainly right as far as it goes, although such stimulation might be more appropriate from the husband rather than herself.

The scriptural authority traditionally cited to support the position, whether Anglican, Roman, or any other, focusing upon the use of the semen, is found in the account of Onan (Genesis 38:8–10) and in St. Paul's condemnation of "effeminates" (I Corinthians 6:9–10).[14] In the second instance, the word translated as "effeminates" is *malakoi,* whose basic root meaning is "soft." The Revised Standard Version joins this word with that which follows, *arsenokoitai,* and renders them both as "homosexuals." Certainly there is much difference between one who masturbates and a homosexual. Whether this translation is justified or not, there does not seem to be any evidence for concluding that *malakoi* refers specifically to those who masturbate.[15]

As regards the story of Onan, which is the more popular authority ("onanism" is a common term for masturbation in Roman Catholic moral theology), this seems to be a mis-application of the text. Onan had failed to fulfill the levirate obligation; namely, to attempt to impregnate the wife of his deceased brother; and it was for this he was condemned. It would appear that what he did was practice *coitus interruptus*, not masturbation.[16] We would hold, therefore, that the Bible says nothing about masturbation.

It is significant that one of the most respected Roman Catholic works dealing with masturbation, *Counseling the Catholic* by Hagmaier and Gleason, at no time cites the Scripture for authority and is at great pains to recognize the complexity of the motives for the act. Infantile mastur-bation is dismissed as normal, and parents are admonished to ignore it.[17] Yet, when the authors are faced with a dis-cussion of adolescent masturbation, it is clear they are caught in a bind. They recognize the almost universal nature of the activity. They acknowledge the unconscious force of the psychosexual development of the individual. But the authority of the Roman Catholic Church will not permit them to admit it as normal, even when the reader feels they would prefer not to accept the "superstitious reverence for semen" upon which it would appear to be built. "The moral theologian is quite right in insisting that masturbation is not, *per se*, an inherent and necessary char-acteristic of human development."[18] Therefore, the door is open to insist that it is a sin.

A real effort is made in this work to take a compassionate approach. Yet the kind of reasoning found here is common to those who want to find an acceptable ground for condemning the practice. No distinction is drawn, for example, between the average adolescent who masturbates and the youth whose compulsive masturbation is a symptom of emotional disturbance. A kind of fuzziness often prevails between the cause and the effect. James Kavanaugh, in commenting on Hagmaier and Gleason's position, speaks of it as "a case of good psychology inhibited by mediocre theology." [19]

An even more recent Roman Catholic study in moral theology, which does not carry an imprimatur, seems to have made the correction for which Kavanaugh calls. Robert O'Neil and Michael Donovan write:

> Masturbation is not an intrinsically evil act. . . . Adolescent masturbation is a "phase-specific sexual activity." . . . It is morally wrong only when it becomes psychologically harmful. . . . Psychologically harmful masturbation is a retardation of psychosexual development, a fixation at the level of autoerotic activity because of anxiety over more mature heterosexual activities. . . . *During the years from the onset of adolescence to about eighteen, occasionally* [sic] *masturbation* (with some periods of more frequency and intensity caused by anxiety) *is statistically, psychologically, and morally normal.* (Italics theirs.) [20]

But an Anglican work of more recent vintage than Bishop Mortimer does not agree and follows the position of Hagmaier and Gleason. Henry Waddams, in *A New Introduction to Moral Theology*, writes:

> Masturbation . . . is not in itself a serious matter, though it must be regarded as undesirable. It is more damaging in its associations than in the act itself, for it is commonly associated with sensual thoughts and imaginary pictures which have a deleterious effect on the personality. . . . It often produces guilt feelings. . . . Failure to overcome the habit sometimes induces in young people neuroses and breakdown in other moral questions. [21]

Again we see emotional disturbance attributed to masturbation, without ever struggling with the question of whether masturbation is an effect more than a cause.

Waddams also introduces a point about the accompanying fantasy, which is likewise found in the discussion of masturbation by the Lutheran theologian Helmut Thielicke. Thielicke astutely points out that the Roman Catholic obsession with the ejaculation of semen separates the act from the intention and is another illustration of the Roman adherence to an "untenable doctrine of works." [22] But he raises three objections to masturbation, which all partake of this question of fantasy so frequently associated with masturbation. He says masturbation is wrong:

> First and above all because in masturbation sex is separated from the I–Thou relationship and thus loses its meaning. . . . Second, because the sexual phantasy is no longer bound to a real partnership and therefore roves about vagrantly. Third, because as a rule absence of this bond leads to physical and psychic extravagance. [23]

This is to say that the only appropriate ejaculation is one associated with a real partner, presumably one's wife, as it is set within the total coital experience. It is the absence of a partner, and the subsequent fantasy, that makes masturbation sinful.

We now see, in moving from an original concern for semen and Onan, that the argument centers itself, among such theologians as Hagmaier, Gleason, Waddams, and Thielicke, about two points: masturbation leads to neurotic behavior, and it promotes a dangerous life of fantasy. We might examine these two points as we look at what psychiatry says about the subject.

Writing in the *Medical Tribune* concerning masturbation, Dr. Walter Stokes states: "We would defend it and recognize the importance it has in any rational concept of personality structure and social relations." [24] Just what he means by this may be better understood in statements such as these:

> In various degrees masturbation is a normal phenomenon from the first year of life up to the time a marital relation is established. . . . In order to function sexually men and women need to have some feeling developed in the genital area. Masturbation is an aid in bringing feeling to that area and centering it in the sexual organs.[25]

> In addition to the simple discharge of sexual tension, masturbation serves such purposes as the reduction of anxiety, expression of hostility, fantasying of sexual experimentation, and assertion of sexual identity in anticipation or recall.[26]

> Moderate amounts of masturbation are therefore considered to be of importance to the development of the sense of self in adolescence.[27]

It would be possible to add many more opinions like this, but the point is made. Masturbation is seen in the psychiatric world as a normal, positive aspect of the psychosexual development of man.

"There is no established medical evidence that masturbation, regardless of frequency, leads to mental illness." [28] My own suspicion is that the absence of masturbation in the history of a person often coincides with an inability to relate effectively in a heterosexual relationship. At least in one particular case study of my own I know this to have been true.

There is no doubt that much guilt is associated with masturbation, and this can be a debilitating factor in the life of an individual. But the cause of this is the severe disapproving attitude of authority figures (such as clergy) or peer groups—a value judgment placed upon what is essentially a normal activity. This is why there seems to be something almost vicious in the attitude of theologians who condemn masturbation as "linked to depression, insecurity, a lack of confidence in self, . . . an undue preoccupation with guilt and sin, and, above all, an inability to give sex and love." [29] Is it not more likely that what is "linked" to these troubles is the judgmental attitude of the Church, which makes a sin out of what is inevitable and normal?

The fantasy commonly associated with masturbation raises a more sophisticated psychological question. Rhoda Lorand is getting at the crux of the matter, however, when she says that one positive contribution of masturbation "is the bringing of the young individual closer to contact with a member of the opposite sex through 'experimental quasi-action in fantasy.'" [30] This is a step in the psychosexual development of the individual, and its *absence* in mastur-batory activity, Mrs. Lorand states, is evidence of emotional difficulty.[31] To understand what she and other psychiatrists are saying we must realize that fantasy—daydreaming, as we sometimes call it—is a vital part of the preparation, not only in the young child but in the adolescent and older person as well, for future experience. It is how he meets the new with some degree of confidence. Even Hagmaier and Gleason recognize this truth of psychology:

> A reasonable amount of daydreaming is a very necessary ingredient for psychological growth. The adolescent, espe-cially, imagines in fantasy future activities which at the moment are not possible or permitted to him. However, there is a limit beyond which such "fantasy living" is not healthy.[32]

It is just this point that Waddams and, more particularly, Thielicke seem to miss. If we are to be prepared for a truly creative I–Thou relationship, fantasy is necessary. Other-wise we will meet the experience of marriage quite unequipped. If we are to bring an identity to the marriage bed (the failure to achieve this is a root cause of marital breakdown), then we need to see the vital role of fantasy in accomplishing an identity.

So we discover that the arguments of the theologians in regard to the psychogenic role of masturbation and the unhealthy effects of the consequent sexual fantasy are directly countered by the insights of psychiatry. Of course, it is possible to argue with these conclusions. There is no doubt that masturbation is part of the pattern found in some very unhealthy people. William Stringfellow says:

> . . . one who persists into adulthood in the practice of masturbation is likely to be one who remains profoundly immature sexually, fearing actual sexual contact with a partner, becoming and being sexually retarded. The main danger and damage in masturbation is not in the conduct itself, but in the fantasy life that invariably accompanies the conduct. That life will hardly ever be a sexually identifying and fulfilling one, and indeed masturbation is probably most obviously another variety of sexual sublimation, one in which the sexual identity and capability of the person remains stalemated, indefinite, confused, and apparently self-contained.[33]

Mrs. Lorand outlines three areas of concern in masturbatory activity. Masturbation can be an escape from reality and can cause difficulties in selecting a suitable partner; it can be an escape from homosexuality, and when the accompanying fantasies are of an extreme masochistic or sadistic nature, it can reveal a very unhealthy psychosexual development.[34]

When these questions are raised, however, it becomes a matter of distinguishing between a positive, normal psychosexual pattern and one that is symptomatic of personality disorder. It is similar to the distinction between fellatio that is a perfectly normal option in the foreplay between a man and wife and fellatio that is, in fact, a perversion. For too long the Church has been unwilling to face this. Certainly there is a "fixated" form of masturbation that is unhealthy. Indeed, adult masturbation can be indicative of a pathological condition or of a failure to achieve sexual identity, both needing our ministry and sometimes that of a psychiatrist. Falling back on masturbation when depressed or frightened is a common experience—for that matter, the same feeling can be the reason for sexual intercourse. But all masturbatory activity cannot be included under such headings. More is positive than destructive in such activity. This is to say that I would agree with Hettlinger's conclusion in his excellent chapter on the subject. He writes: "It seems to me that the Christian should be able to accept this outlet thankfully. . . ." [35]

However, I also recognize that the mind of the Church is not going to take this attitude simply because we refute the arguments of those opposed. I am reminded of opinions expressed in preliminary discussions of this study. One very fine, psychologically aware priest, when faced with the substantial opinion that the Bible says nothing about masturbation, remarked: "I don't care what the scholars say, Onan masturbated, and that is that!" At a clergy conference discussing the issue, such fear was raised at the possibility of the acceptance of masturbation among adolescents that it was suggested that those present vote on whether or not it was a sin. We have to see that masturbation is tied up with a larger guilt and anxiety that we (and the Church for two thousand years) associate with sex and that manifests itself in essentially an *emotional* conviction that our sexual organs are dirty and what they do is nasty.

When we have faced this heritage and dealt with it on the emotional level, we might be prepared to cope with masturbation, particularly as it occurs in adolescents. Let us not think that we shall encourage masturbation by such an attitude. Our adolescents are going to masturbate no matter how we feel about it. But let us hope that by dealing with it openly and realistically we can make it as positive a force in their lives as possible.

When someone in confession or during counseling speaks of masturbation, what should we do? First, we should determine the pattern of masturbation. Is it regressive? What is the nature of the masturbatory fantasies? How does it fit into the total identity of the individual (i.e., what are the possibilities of homosexuality)? If we are led to think that it is a symptom of possible psychopathy, then maybe we need to suggest further assistance. More than likely such a symptom is not indicated. Second, we should explore the guilt associated with masturbation and the total view of the confessee's or counselee's sexuality without reinforcing the frequent conviction that he is committing a horrible sin. This exploration should lead into all kinds of areas not appropriate to the confessional (if that is where we have started) and, therefore, should always involve counseling. The counseling should include the whole pattern of the person's understanding of his identity, the kind of image he is getting from his parents, and the manner in which he perceives human sexuality. The clergyman himself needs to relate to the counselee as a sane, healthy male, capable of creative sexuality; and yet as a person who, far more likely than not, has masturbated himself (although perhaps this need not be said in so many words).

What I am pleading for is, first of all, self-understanding on the part of the pastor, coupled with a solid theology of sex. Secondly, I ask for psychological awareness, devoid of intruding fears and guilts on our own part. Then, I suggest, we shall be prepared to deal with the sick and the healthy, both of whom we may assume masturbate.

* 6 *

SEX EDUCATION
AND THE CHURCH

MUCH has been written in the past few years on the subject of sex education. It has been honored by a *Time* editorial [1] and taught in graduate seminars in our most eminent universities. Since the fall of 1968 the subject has earned the wrath of those organizations generally believed to represent the extreme right, and consequently, it has become a controversial subject argued in the halls of Congress and the state legislatures.[2] It is something upon which a great many people have rather strong opinions at present, and it is extremely difficult sometimes to predict who will be in favor and who will be opposed.

We say this by way of a preface, both to explain why we cannot offer in this one chapter a complete outline of how to carry out a program of sex education and to warn the enthusiastic clergyman or lay leader about entering into such a program in his parish without laying a careful groundwork among all who will be touched by it. Yet, for reasons we trust are obvious not only in this chapter but throughout the book, we would also insist that the Church has an active role in sex education.

I. THE SOURCE OF SEX EDUCATION

Appropriately and inevitably, sex education begins with parents; and this can be the very root of our problem. It begins as soon as a child is born, and perhaps even before.[3]

If this appears to be a puzzling statement, remember our definition of "sex" and "sexuality" (as well as "gender") and recall our repeated insistence that we learn our character traits (that is, those that are not inherited) through identification first with parents, then with siblings, and after that with teachers and peers. Consequently, it is pointless to attack formal sex education in the school or the church on the grounds that it intentionally seeks to usurp what belongs in the home. Short of a radical break with our present form of socialization, there is no need to argue that question. What is in question, rather, is whether the home provides all that is needed.

It might help at this point if we distinguished in sex education between "attitudes" and "information." Attitudes comprise the values, morals, and feelings that underlie our behavior. Information refers to our factual knowledge of the nature and function of the human reproductive system, both anatomically and psychologically. Information is not, as far as we can discover, determinative of behavior; and to think so is to commit the so-called Socratic fallacy (education necessarily begets moral behavior). We are convinced that attitudes are the important thing, and we believe with John Gagnon that they are learned primarily from our parents.[4] He also tells us that "in all American studies it is clear that the primary source of sex information [as distinct from attitudes] is peers."[5] Perhaps this is as it should be. Are not parents the inevitable and rightful teachers of sexual attitudes? We have also been asked on occasion, "What is wrong with a little misinformation from 'behind the barn'?"

In regard to the first question, we have to acknowledge that parents today are relatively ignorant about sex.[6] From experience relative to this study, we have discovered that efforts to explore the meaning of femininity and masculinity with educated audiences frequently meets with confusion, hostility, and flight. They find it very difficult to deal with the subject beyond fantasies concerning the sexual behavior of real or imagined adolescents. Yet, as we maintain in this study, understanding the nature or ontology of Man is the very heart of developing healthy attitudes concerning our sexuality. Charles Goldsmith, a pastor, clinical psychologist, and leader in the Association of Clinical Pastoral Education, has repeatedly expressed his conviction based upon extensive professional experience that the fundamental problem in our society today is confusion as to the meaning of masculinity and femininity.[7] This is confirmed by the obvious fact that few people even know what the words mean.

Having said this, we must add our impression that even among married adults sexual information can be grossly inadequate. Any pastoral counselor experienced in administering the "Sex Knowledge Inventory" (SKI, see section on premarital counseling, p. 98) knows that a surprising number of men with wide coital experience have only a dim idea of what is happening. Members of what a friend of mine aptly titled "The Post-Ruskin Society" (i.e., those who abrogate technology and embrace as a cultic act homemade bread, goat's milk, and outdoor privies) will protest that this is all well and good, because it adds to the "mystery." I would agree with Leslie Farber that we do not wish to reduce coitus to a clinical performance;[8] but that is not all that can be said. I recall a man in his thirties who, when counseling with me, firmly rejected the idea that he might be failing his wife by seeking coitus only three or four times a year, and then with absolutely no foreplay, when he was awakened at 2:00 A.M. by an erotic dream. Although his problem was obviously deeper than this, would not a little information have been helpful here?

Most important of all, many adults not only possess a narrow vision of human sexuality and a minimum of correct information, but the whole subject is anxiety-laden to an unbelievable degree for them. At a PTA meeting, in the "Question and Answer" period after a talk on sexuality, I recall a woman asking me with shaking voice and trembling hands, "How can we keep our children from sinning if we don't teach them when they are little that sex is dirty and filthy?" I was not surprised to learn later from the principal that her son had been recently discharged from the service on a psychiatric disability. A bill to severely limit sex education was put before the Education Committee of the Wisconsin State Assembly. At the hearing, the members of the committee not only were told that sex education was a "Communist plot" but were asked, rhetorically, why children had to be taught the sex act while animals did not.[9] What kind of marriage is it where human sexuality is reduced to the level of a rutting season?

These incidents are characteristic of the person who is very afraid of losing control of his environment, of his own emotions, and consequently of his very life. They testify to the power of sex, that it becomes a "peg" upon which the anxious person "hangs his fears"; fears that are often inchoate and of uncertain origin.[10] In other words, what a parent conveys to his child about things sexual is often merely an expression of his own desperate struggle to maintain an identity and some contact with reality in the face of internal needs he little understands. His panic before the so-called sexual revolution, his rejection of his own sexuality, and his unrealistic and rigid sexual morality very often express a real emotional upset of a much broader scope. The tragedy is that it is precisely in such a home that the sexual "acting out," which such a person imagines of all young people, comes true and reinforces his crusade to restore a repressive society and a Victorian sexuality.[11]

It is in this climate that we can all acknowledge that sexual attitudes are indeed learned from the parents, and join with the lament of Mary Calderone:

> We are confronted with an almost impossible situation, in which the sexual crippling of the adult portion of the population almost automatically and inevitably passes itself on as a crippling force to the growing young person.[12]

A few years ago, Paul H. Gebhard made a study of the sex education of sex offenders. We have every reason to believe that the personality disorders that produced this behavior had their roots in the family; but Gebhard also established the fact that 75 per cent of these men received no sex information from their parents.[13] We suspect that the kind of parent who raises a sex offender is the kind who is also threatened by outside sex education, protests the fact that he can impart the information himself, and, in fact, does not. Truly, we doubt that most parents do. Gagnon, as we have stated, makes it clear that he believes such information comes primarily from peers; and our informal polls from place to place would certainly reinforce both Gebhard's figure and Gagnon's claim.

But is this to be expected and accepted? Prior to puberty (about age 12) a child in an open home will, more often than not, readily discuss matters of sex information with his parents. This is, of course, after he has reached an age when he can conceptualize such questions, and only when the questions arise naturally from his own wondering.[14] It is important that our answers be direct and honest and that we do not attempt to tell the child more than he wants to know. It also assumes an *open* home (which we have already indicated is not as common as we would like to think) and parents who know the information (again, not something of which we can be sure). But once the child reaches the age of puberty it seems that by the very nature of the adolescent process there comes a separation between parent and child, which involves among many other things the ability to discuss explicitly matters of sex information. This is particularly true because we find here a renewal of the Oedipal crisis and the subsequent devaluation of the parents to counter this; which would focus itself in strongly conflicted feelings about the parents as sexual persons.[15]

Gertrude Couch, in a survey of some Detroit young people, reported:

> Parents were identified often for the first choice, if not the major source of sex guidance *in the early years*. . . . But an almost universal complaint was that *parents were not able to or did not do* an adequate job.[16]

This would appear to illustrate, on the one hand, the inevitable guilt the adolescent feels about his parents ("we wish that our parents were 'the major source for sex guidance' "), but on the other hand, the fact is that there is no communication in most cases.

Certainly in working with junior high students we have been asked the kind of questions that would indicate again and again the inability of parents and young adolescents to talk about sex—information or attitudes. These are examples of questions actually asked by seventh graders in a public school: "Doesn't it hurt to have intercourse?" "If women have small breasts, do they still produce milk?" "How come people feel embarrassed when we talk about sex organs?" "Why do they circumcise?" "How many times can you masturbate?"[17] These questions seem to have in common a color of anxiety, even though they are not matters in which you could read misconduct; yet they were asked of teachers and *not of parents!*

If it is true, as we believe it is, that at the time the child reaches puberty the parent generally ceases to be the main source of sex information and the explicit clarification of attitudes, does it necessarily follow that the church, school, or some other social agency should attempt to take over? In other words, "What is wrong with a little misinformation from 'behind the barn'?" It could be argued in reply that haphazard peer information might not answer correctly the kind of questions we have just read, and in consequence, a person's anxiety might be deepened needlessly; in fact, real tragedy could ensue. Frank Furstenberg and his associates offer evidence that illegitimacy in this country is *not* related to promiscuity, but rather to *lack of information* about birth control.[18] There is nothing to be gained by some sort of retributive attitude that such is the just fruit of the teenager's sin. Rather we have a case in point where responsible sex education can minister to a critical social problem, not to mention alleviate much personal anxiety.

This, together with the more positive hope that through correct sexual information we can prepare people for a happier marriage, is an adequate reason for a program of sex education outside the home. Far more important, however, is our conviction that you cannot divorce sexual information from attitudes that give birth to morality, that you cannot demand of the adolescent that his ethical development be rooted solely in the home. Adolescence is a time for working through various trial ideologies so that the individual emerges with an adult ethical sense.[19] Now for the first time he has the intellectual ability to do this,[20] and of necessity, he must do it primarily outside the family.[21] Not only his peers, but every adult with whom he has close contact becomes a party to this kind of clarification. John Wilson, Norman Williams, and Barry Sugarman, in a study of the process of moral education, conclude that without doubt "we are all moral educators, whether we like it or not," [22] and we have a responsibility to our young people to provide a responsible context for this in our school systems.[23] For this reason, above all, we particularly urge sex education in the schools (especially from the seventh grade on), in the churches, and in other responsible social agencies.

II. The Church's Role in Sex Education

We have said that sexuality is an emotionally charged subject, a clue to the inner life of the total person. This can be as true for clergy and lay leaders of the Church as for anyone else. For example: recently the newspapers carried the announcement of the forming of a Roman Catholic group called "Credo," for the purpose, among others, of supporting the "concern of many parents over sex education programs due to the very clinical approach without stressing moral principles and the infringement of their parental rights in this extremely personal area." [24] Since, as we have shown, this statement is in conflict with what can be said on at least two counts, we assume that it reflects an emotional "set" already described. We would have to say the same of the clergyman who dismissed the Church's role in this area with the incredibly hostile statement, "I know *nothing* about sex!" (His two children were standing by at the time.) The question we would and did ask was, "How can the Church minister to the person and say it knows nothing about sex?"

Fr. Louis Hanlon writes: "More than anything else adolescents need a *theology* of sex. By a theology of sex I mean an understanding of sex which relates it to their vocation as Christians." [25] Fr. Lester Kinsolving, in an article in *Sex Education and the Teenager*, says: "What seems desperately needed is a clear concept and realization of the theology of sex." [26] Our study is one effort to meet just this need, and it is predicated upon the assumption that all sex education must be rooted in an understanding of man as a sexual person; and that the Church consequently not only has a role, but *the fundamental role* to play in this.

Much of what has been written in the field of sex education has seen the Church as essentially an "expediter" of public school programs[27] and the clergy as agents of referral to medical doctors, marriage counselors, and psychologists. We think that whereas we can serve these functions when the occasion seems to demand, it would be a grave error to limit ourselves in this way. Our basic reason for saying this may be seen in what Frs. Hanlon and Kinsolving see so clearly: that the understanding of sexuality must be set in a broad theological context. It is my experience that many people who are committed to sex education find themselves ill at ease outside of a biological framework, much less in discussing the matter in its theological ramifications. It is also true that not everyone can talk of sexual matters in an anxiety-free manner, and this can often be true of physicians—as well as teachers and counselors. For clergy, whose calling demands of them an openness to the intimate lives of others, sexuality should be accessible to honest discourse.

Another very practical reason why the Church ought to be "stage center" in programs of sex education is that the real need is for an *adult* program.[28] As we have said, parents are the primary source of sex education; but parents are too often both ignorant and anxious. We cannot foresee any radical change in the process of socialization. For us, then, the obvious answer is to concentrate on creating an informed and relaxed adult constituency capable of bringing up children with a creative sense of their own sexuality. Perhaps this sounds a little utopian, but solid beginnings are made of such dreams. Who can reach adults in such matters as these in greatest breadth and depth? The answer in our society is still the Church; for that reason we would heartily endorse any attempt of our congregations to involve themselves in effective programs of this kind.

When the Church accepts some direct responsibility toward sex education, we often handle our unresolved anxieties about the subject by restricting ourselves to discussing only the "spiritual meaning of sexuality." This persistent Cartesian trap, for which we Christians have a distressing disposition, really will not do. We cannot talk about sex without talking about penises, vaginas, and orgasms anymore than we can discuss its physical dimensions without touching on its meaning to the whole person. We can understand Fr. Capon's plea, in his excellent little book *Bed and Board*, that we stay away from the "marriage manual approach" to sex education.[29] We would agree that good technique is not the key to happy marriages and that there is more meaning to coitus than a mutual orgasm. But when we still have adults who think that masturbation turns your brain to jelly, that the male can render himself sterile by taking a good hot bath, and that a clitoris is part of a sailing vessel, then there is purpose in the marriage manual and a reason for the careful explanation of physiology and technique even to the long-married.[30]

Of course, this responsibility lies primarily with the clergyman and requires two things of him. First of all, he has to possess the basic knowledge of the physiology and psychology of sex, which is not very difficult to acquire. Some of the books listed in the Bibliography can provide it. Second, he needs to be sensitive to his own unconscious feelings about this subject and to find the ability to talk about it without threat. This is probably much harder to achieve and is the reason why some clergy will avoid the responsibility by pleading ignorance.

The Church also has a particular responsibility to young people, as well as to adults, and they are a secondary target for our program of sex education. Ideally, this is a role that supplements what is being done in the schools and is built upon what has already gone on between the parents and the young person. Its focus is, therefore, *the clarification of values in terms of a distinctively Christian theology of sexuality and its moral implications.*[31] This is something that we cannot expect of the schools in a pluralistic society, and that can best be done in a group setting by outsiders, apart from home and parents. Of course, where a school program is lacking and/or where parents have failed, the Church must do its best to make up for the lack. This is very difficult to do, particularly in cases of parental failure. The Church cannot expect to have a radical influence in changing behavior already rooted in an unhealthy home situation.

A word of warning might be appropriate here. When Church youth programs are flagging, there is a tradition of building them back with a series on "sex." This is using sex for ulterior motives and generally fools no one. It says all the wrong things. As a matter of fact, adults tend to overemphasize adolescent preoccupation with sexuality, largely as a result of their own anxieties and projection. Whereas Earl Brill's confident obituary for sex might be a little premature, it is true that "in recent years there has been a marked decline in the traditional preoccupation of college students with sex" [32]—and it seems to have infected the high school as well.

III. Toward a Methodology

Despite the partial truth of the claim that the family is no longer *the* primary community in America, and in the face of predictions of the imminent demise of the parish, it appears still true that the Church relates first of all to family structures and that the average clergyman is a family specialist in his teaching and counseling. His primary tools in this work are himself as a person of Christian integrity and his willingness to enter into dialogue with others.

We believe the best context for effectiveness in this area is the small group. We would certainly not want to disclaim the value of the sermon or even to suggest that a lecture is never appropriate; but we cannot foresee a truly helpful program of sex education—among either adults or adolescents—that does not utilize the kind of dialogue possible within a group of 8 to 12 people, where not only information can be more effectively communicated, but feelings can be perceived and shared. What we discuss here is, therefore, always in the context of small group work in some sense (even if only a group of three). We shall not, however, attempt to teach small group methods. Guides for this can be found in various excellent books.[33] It can also become a part of an individual's skills only through participation in groups, and the practice of leadership under supervision.

But we are very much aware that there is some lack of specific guidance for clergy and lay leaders of the Church in adult sex education. Books and pamphlets have been published on premarital counseling, but they are either out of print, poor in quality, or generally do not address themselves to the situation in which the average parish clergy and lay leaders find themselves.[34] Literature on marriage counseling is likewise not always precisely what is needed.[35] Our intention here is to sketch in outline form some possibilities for a teaching and counseling ministry with adults, in the hope that clergy may be encouraged to acquire the implied skills and knowledge through further reading and practice under supervision.

Premarital Instruction

Many churches require or at least recommend some premarital instruction. This, of course, ought to be of the most competent and fullest kind possible. Unfortunately, most laymen are totally unaware of the requirements of their churches in this matter and much less cognizant of the responsibility of the clergyman in assisting their entrance into this strange, new life of holy matrimony. There is great need for explaining this to them, for suitable publication of the Church's position, and for courage in maintaining it. *We cannot permit ourselves to be rushed into inadequate instruction.*

Perhaps the best opportunity for sex education of adults in depth can take place in premarital instruction. This, of course, implies an understanding of sexuality in its broad sense (see chapter 1); and means education not only in coital behavior, but in the theological implications of masculinity and femininity as worked out in the daily communication of a married couple.

We will offer two rather different approaches—at least on the surface they appear different—to premarital instruction. Our reason for this is that we believe the method employed depends in part on the personality of the priest, and these two outlines are attempts to achieve the same end with a different technique.

First of all, in very brief form, is a pattern of instruction tested with well over a hundred couples as it evolved at St. Alban's Episcopal Chapel at Louisiana State University, Baton Rouge, Louisiana. It was always carried out with the couple and the priest alone in an informal and relaxed manner. Dialogue was encouraged, disagreement welcomed, and honesty required. (We must admit that in the midst of it some people decided *not* to get married; but at least the subsequent divorce rate was not noticeably increased.)

Preliminary meeting: Not part of the instruction *per se*, the first meeting is arranged in response to a phone call from the engaged couple requesting an interview. At this interview it is determined whether or not you will undertake the instruction and wedding. Ask three questions first of all: *"Are you both baptized?"* [36] *"Has either of you ever been married before?"* (Do not fail to ask this question! Often the information is not volunteered.) And (to the prospective bride) *"Are you pregnant?"* [37] Then, if you decide to accept the task, get the wedding details out of the way—flowers, date, music, attendants, rings, license, medical appointment (both the bride and the groom should have a complete examination, not just the blood test required by the state), etc. These matters of parish administration should not be allowed to intrude upon the priest's teaching function. This is a time to give them what literature you wish to distribute. We would recommend giving them Donald Hasting's *A Doctor Speaks on Sexual Expression in Marriage*, and Robert Capon's *Bed and Board*. Also give them now any sort of printed statement of what the Church and the local parish expect of them by virtue of the fact that they are getting married by you in that parish. You conclude this meeting with an explanation of the instruction required and set up the proper time or times (depending on circumstances and the time available).

First session: This is devoted to the *theology of marriage.* First attraction in our society is based upon "cardiorespiratory" love (your heart beats faster and your breath gets shorter). Talk about Christian love, which is not just *giving*, but *sharing* some areas of mutual concern (enough to allow communication) and also frankly acknowledging the *need for the other*. Here masculinity and femininity should be described—as it truly is *and* as our society erroneously conceives it.[38] The sacramental principle as the means of effecting the image of God through our sexuality (see chapter 1) is then discussed.

Second session: At this time administer the "Sex Knowledge Inventory" (SKI). This is obtainable through Family Life Publications, P. O. Box 6725, Durham, North Carolina, 27708. You do not have to be present for this (a secretary can do it); however, you should get the couple's permission to give them the test, and explain its purpose in advance. It is *not* a projection test, which frightens some people. It rather seeks to uncover areas of inadequate information and attitude. The test must be taken separately by the bride and the groom.

Third session: Having examined their SKI, the priest now has a basis for discussing the Christian understanding of human sexuality. Often there is resistance to this on the part of the man (rarely the woman), and the SKI has the great value of gaining interest. The priest should be very familiar with the manual that comes with the SKI. But he should carry his discussion far beyond physiology and attitudes to the whole question of the theological significance of intercourse. This is the time also to discuss the matter of birth control.

Fourth session: This will probably be the longest interview because you will wish to discuss areas of communication beyond the immediate coital involvement, such as money, children, decision making, etc. We strongly recommend that the priest obtain the "Marriage Counseling Kit" from the McKinley Foundation, 809 S. 5th Street, Champaign, Illinois. This consists of a set of cards with statements about attitudes toward marriage. It provides the couple with an opportunity to compare their opinions with one another, with a competent psychologist (who gives his response on the opposite side of each card), and with the pastor. It provokes a natural and honest conversation about all kinds of areas of concern (e.g., money, table manners, number of children, authority, etc.), into which the priest may enter or not as the occasion indicates. This will take two hours at least.

Fifth session: The last appointment can be devoted to "creed and cult," the family's religious life, the marriage service itself (its meaning, not what you do), the importance of the Church to a marriage. (For Episcopalians, this is also the time to sign the Declaration of Intention, required by Canon Law.) All "loose ends" can be caught up here. If we burden the couple with too much specific advice, it is possible that they will forget the important things in the plethora of detail. But some specific questions might be put to them concerning themselves, and this can be handled now.

A second method of premarital instruction, which we might call the "encounter" technique, has been developed over a good number of years and is now used at St. Luke's Episcopal Church in Bethesda, Maryland. Its real difference from the first method is that the structure of the counseling emerges from the process of the various sessions themselves (there is no outline of particular material to be covered at a given time), feelings such as those of anger are encouraged, and consequently *the maturity and counseling skill of the clergyman must be firmly established.*

Basically, three sessions of an hour-and-a-half to two hours are required. More might be added as they seem needed. The first session concentrates on the "interview," by which is meant "the simple process of allowing counselees to tell the counselor and one another about themselves." However, the interview continues in some sense throughout the counseling. The goal of this relationship is to get the man and woman to face their own feelings and values and those of each other—many of which have undoubtedly gone unsaid—and to deal with them honestly. This kind of communication and realistic insight into the other is the "stuff" of which creative marriages are made and is, in the mind of those who do this, the best kind of "instruction" the Church can give.

Needless to say, the process starts on a low key and works up to a high pitch of feeling. The quotations that follow were taken from a report on this method given to us personally by the Rev. Roy S. Turner, rector of St. Luke's Church:

> The encounter builds on the material coming out of the interview and leads toward dialogue. I sometimes take us to encounter by asking them what they feel about something the other has said about himself or herself. Sometimes it is brought on by challenging one or the other of them, or both directly, as to a feeling or the absence of it. Sometimes I ask them to recall the last heated argument they had and to describe how they felt about it and how they feel about it now. When it seems useful I also ask for descriptions of other emotional encounters. For example, if the couple has been having sexual intercourse, I inquire about it, about their concerns, fears, and such like. I use a note pad to jot down important points for later use. If I notice places where the counselee is embarrassed, hesitant or anxious to talk about himself or herself, I note it and encourage or challenge them to return to it later.

Obviously, the raw exchange of feelings—hostile or otherwise—has little value *in itself*. There must be reflection upon this, and conversation about what has been felt and said must take place.

> Toward the end of the premarital counseling, the information that is fed begins to include material from the marriage

canons, the marriage service, and data from our general social situation in which the marriage will continue. Normally, the couple will now be ready to benefit from some such help.

Clearly one of the purposes of this method is to teach a couple not to be afraid of fights, but to fight fairly and creatively. But beyond this, it is also designed to evoke some perception of their values—that in which they have invested themselves—or what they think are their values; to experience confrontation with the values of the priest; and to discover adequate reasons for their own or for changing them. In this emphasis upon encounter, feeling, values, reflection, and possible change, we have a method that incorporates some of the most current insights into the process of helpful counseling.[39] My only caveat is an important one and needs to be repeated. This method should not be tried by anyone who does not understand his own feelings or who is not trained in this kind of emotion-charged conversation.

Routine Early Marital Counseling

One of the problems implicit in premarital counseling is that unless the couple has already "set up housekeeping" much of the conversation can border on the "academic." Furthermore, there can also be a rather romantic aura pervading the whole process (no matter how blunt and honest the counselor), which wet stockings on the shower door, rollers on the pillow, and soiled shirts on the floor will yet subdue. Also, premarital counseling in many churches is generally done, either by design or happenstance, in groups of three couples—a practice we would personally want to maintain.

We have discovered, therefore, the great values in organizing within the parish a group of people, married a year or two, who gather under the leadership of the priest simply to discuss marriage in general and their own in particular.[40] The purpose of this is, again, the exploration of feelings and values, the opening of people to information that they might not otherwise be able to hear, and the support of a trusted and loving community for what in fact is a traumatic time in life. It is our experience that a sensitive leader need only introduce a subject—in-laws, nocturnal interruptions by the new baby, money and working wives, role relationships, etc.—and the conversation flows.

As an example of what can happen, here is a short, though very interesting exchange between three couples: a lapsed Roman Catholic and a Lutheran convert to Roman Catholicism (couple *A*); two Episcopalians (couple *B*); a devout Roman Catholic and a Jew taking Roman Catholic instruction (couple *C*). None of the couples had met each other before and none of them knew the priest-counselor. They came together for the first time in this group, and the whole session was relaxed, extremely open, and expressive. They were discussing premarital intercourse and the wedding night, and Husband *B* had just explained why he believed in "trial marriage."

> *Husband A:* I'd like to say one thing about this wedding night deal. . . . Since we did have premarital sex, when our wedding night came this was . . . this was *something* for us. You know, not only the fact that . . . um . . . well, you know, we were married. This is where we could say, "O.K., now the whole arrangement is done and finished with."
>
> *Wife A:* "We're legal!" [She had previously referred just in passing to an illegitimate child, apparently by someone else.]
>
> *Husband A:* No, no; it wasn't all just being "legal." It was

just about something "there." Since we had [intercourse] before, we knew each other and knew what each other wanted. And . . . I don't know . . . you know, it's something that's hard to explain; but there was something "there" then that set it aside. It's one special night for us!

Wife A: It [having premarital intercourse] made it all the more special for me . . . all the more beautiful!

Husband A: Yeah!

Wife B: It's not, "What on earth is he going to do?" [It never became explicit what couple *B*'s experience had been in this area.]

Husband A: Right!

Wife B: Should I or should I not go dressed or undressed [to bed]? Should I go into the bathroom to get dressed or should he? . . ." [Much talking at once, much laughter.]

Husband C: We had two separate bathrooms. [More laughter.]

Wife C: For us, we knew each other for about five and a half years before we got married. [She had already told us of problems with "nerves," attacks of colitis, etc.]

Husband C: Six and a half!

Wife C: For me . . . maybe it was just the way I was . . . I was . . . brought up; I just had this feeling that when I got married that was the time and the place for sex, and not before. I admit that I was the first one to turn over and go to sleep on my wedding night. I was so tired, I couldn't see straight; and I was scared to death. . . . [Laughter.] I just turned over and went to sleep, and . . .

Priest: How did your husband feel about that?

Husband C: I watched television.

Wife C: I don't think he was too happy with me. But . . . uh . . . I don't know . . . I think that we . . . being that we're married and mean so much more to each other now . . . and I think this says something for it [waiting for intercourse], too. You can learn together, instead of . . . it . . . to me it means more when you're married than before you're married. I've always [tape unintelligible] . . . that it is something very sacred, and goes with marriage.

There is a great deal of thought-provoking material in this short conversation, which could provide many helpful insights that we cannot now explore. For our immediate purposes we need only point out the spirit of communication found in this paradigm of the routine marital counseling group, the opportunity it afforded for the expression of feelings and the examination of values and commitment. Such a group can be organized in any parish of reasonable size with four or five couples, married for no more, say, than two years. When a couple reaches their second anniversary, they can drop out and another can come in. When the size of a given parish is too small, there is no reason why, in this ecumenical age, we cannot draw from other congregations, as the group described here did. The rewards from this, we believe, can be as great as anything we do in family counseling. In the first year or two, where the marital relationship and the relationship to the first child (often now anticipated or arrived) are being forged, crucial patterns of living can be established with guidance of a kind that can be understood and used.

Special Programs of Marital Education

It will not be our purpose to discuss in this study methods of counseling marriages in crisis. Our goals here are more pedagogical than therapeutic, more preventative than curative.[41] What I would now briefly outline are two very different ways of approaching some special efforts at developing freer and more creative sexual relationships.

First of all, the important thing in educating persons in

sexuality is to expose feelings and to provide opportunities for reappraisal. This requires a certain expertise on the part of the leadership, which is not always readily available. Is there another approach, a "second best" that would be better than nothing? Is there some sort of program where information could be fed in, and to which some group response could be made? We are speaking of the possibility of a prestructured, less spontaneous approach to adult sex education that will allow something to happen, but not more than the leadership can handle.

We have had experience in programs that over a period of weeks presented a series of speakers—a doctor, a psychologist, a judge or social worker, a clergyman—talking for thirty minutes on their particular insights regarding sexuality. The lecture would be followed by small group discussions in which a chance was given for personal responses. Questions would be formulated out of these sessions, and the program would conclude each evening with a large group discussion, led by the speaker.

A possible alternative to this general outline is provided by the Family Enrichment Bureau of Escanaba, Michigan. Under the direction of Urban Steinmetz, a marriage counselor long associated with the Church, this organization has recorded a series of twelve talks (usually about thirty minutes in length), divided into six sessions. They deal with such subjects as married love, communication, sexual enjoyment, family planning, money, and sex education. The whole thing is called the *Marriage Enrichment Program*, and the album with manual may be obtained from the Family Enrichment Bureau, 1615 Ludington Street, Escanaba, Michigan, 49829, for $37.50.

These records provide an informed opinion and, especially in small towns, they are more readily available and easier to schedule than speakers—doctor, psychologist, etc. —as in the first example. They are also a "known quantity," and I would describe them as low-key and very safe. However, they seem to me impersonal and "canned" in concept and might be questioned as to general tone and sometimes particular information. Mr. Steinmetz, who does most of the talking, seems to be a rather hyperdevout person (his *repeated* references to "Almighty God" become quite irritating) who is, nevertheless, reasonably well informed in the social and behavioral sciences. His intended audience is probably not very sophisticated and apparently responds well to his pietistic allusions. His style of delivery is rambling, and his manner, when he talks about sex, is most unfortunate. In particular, he considers homosexuality a "dread disease," makes more of mutual orgasm than I think Masters and Johnson would, and has a rather simplistic understanding of Puritans and Jansenists. It seems to me that some of his efforts at "making things simple" result in making them more confusing. Can we simply speak of the clitoris as a "little penis," the erect penis as an "inflated balloon," a pregnant woman as "schizophrenic," and the end of the penis as a "trigger"? I personally object to his use of "sex" (as in "sex intercourse") as an adjective.

Lester Kirkendall, in reviewing a similar program of the Family Enrichment Bureau, *Young Adult Enrichment Program: Sex Education*, objects to some of the same things and suggests that "no formal sex education would be better than this." [42] On the other hand, we would say that one thing does come across loud and clear in these talks, and that is that we are sexual persons, that God made us this way, and that we ought to enjoy it! This is good, and it needs to be said. Perhaps, then, in some parishes and groups where the leadership feels very unsure of itself and wants to be rather cautious, and where the people are generally frightened of their sexuality, this might be better than nothing. It should not be used, however, where the hesitant style, the excessive-piety, the easy distinctions, and the occasional misinformation would become a problem. In using the *Marriage Enrichment Program* the leadership must read widely enough to enter into some dialogue with Mr. Steinmetz and must provide for small group discussion afterwards. They need to point out that the actual physical action of orgasm does not take place as is described here.[43]

At the opposite end of the spectrum there is the kind of training that comes out of the insights of group psychology, as practically developed by such groups as the National Training Laboratories of the National Education Association and the Esalen Institute. Dr. Herbert A. Otto, chairman of the National Center for the Exploration of Human Potential in La Jolla, California, has devised a method of dealing with "sex stereotypes" that inhibit interpersonal communication.[44] This program has been adapted for use in the parish of St. Matthew's Episcopal Church, Kenosha, Wisconsin.[45] It offers trained leadership a context for handling the rather volatile feelings about sexuality (in our broad sense of the word) which we all possess. It is not a course in the mechanics of lovemaking, such as a local doctor or Steinmetz might attempt.

As done at St. Matthew's, this program covers two meetings of a given group meeting once a week. The same idea is adaptable to a twenty-minute exercise for task-oriented groups, such as a parish planning council. The meetings always begin with some sort of nonverbal, tactual communication; and the second session is particularly related to sexual stereotypes.[46]

In the first session, after the nonverbal exercise, the leader discusses with the group the reality of sexual stereotyping. We do not treat the opposite sex as persons, but we put them in "boxes" (e.g., all women are "emotional and irrational"). Since every person is both masculine and feminine (see page 3), it also means we stereotype ourselves. These stereotypes not only express socialized attitudes, but they also contain elements of hostility, fear, anger, and frustration.[47] Added to this are the sexual fantasies that are a part of the motivation of any creative person. When colored by sexual stereotypes, however, they can often lead to guilt, shame, depression, and repression. What needs to happen is that we enjoy our sexual fantasies, learn that they need not be "acted out," and that they do not have to be seen in terms of sexual stereotypes.

Having stated that the object of the exercise is to remove such stereotyping, the leader hands to the women a paper stating: "All men are . . ." He gives to the men one headed: "All women are . . ." They then have five minutes to complete the sentence in as many ways as they can. The papers are collected, and the men read the women's answers out loud, and the women the men's. Two questions are asked: "What is your reaction to this?" and "What effect do our stereotypes have on our functioning as a group?" The session concludes with breaking into groups of four and discussing three more questions: "What does it mean to me that I am a man (or woman)?"; "As such (a man or woman) what do I have to give?"; "What do I want to give?"

The second session begins with a nonverbal exercise, devised by Otto, in which each person selects a partner of the opposite sex, frames the partner's face by putting their hands on his (or her) cheeks, and gazes into the other's eyes for three minutes without speaking.[48] The exercise is then repeated with another partner, after which the experience is discussed in groups of four. Following this there is a lecture on masculinity and femininity, particularly pointing out how these concepts are confused in our society. This leads to a documentation of masculine and feminine competition, starting with the physical aspects and working into the emotional (e.g., stronger vs. weaker; originator vs. receiver; aggressor vs. acceptor; seducer vs. seduced; better sufferer vs. poorer sufferer; objective vs. subjective, *etc.*). Then the large group returns to the small units, and the program is concluded by further discussion, in terms of these polarities, of three questions: "What does it mean to you that you are a man (or a woman)?"; "When do you feel most masculine (or feminine)?"; "What traits, masculine or feminine, do you see yourself having?"

This program is reported as having great success in exposing feelings about sexuality and providing opportunities, as we have suggested is desirable, for their reappraisal. Such a program obviously requires commitment to and training in the kind of sensitivity experience that some find controversial, threatening, or rude. With this and the other program we have outlined, some indication is given of the kind of special offering that the Church can provide for adults.

Programs of Adolescent Education

Our secondary concern for adolescent sex education has undoubtedly received much more programatic attention than adult training. Two courses, still available, which have been widely used are Canon Bryan Green's lectures, "A Basis for Sex Morality" (a six-filmstrip series in color, with script, seven study guides, three records), produced by Cathedral Films (1964); and Charles Batten and Donald McLean's *Fit to Be Tied*, published by Seabury Press (1960).

Canon Green's recorded lectures are, in fact, taken live from a series of talks he gave to some college students. They are, as the title indicates, very concerned with helping unmarried adolescents make a proper moral decision as regards their own sexual behavior. It is done in a humorous, non-moralizing way, and the art work, which is largely diagrammatic and symbolic, is in color and is good. The English accent of Canon Green may make him a little difficult to follow at times. However, the NCC's *Audio-Visual Resources Guide* (8th ed.) rates this series as "highly recommended," if it is followed by discussion (for which guides are provided).

The series, as with the "Marriage Enrichment Program," is helpful if the parish needs a prestructured, somewhat "canned" approach to this field. It does not free the leader from talking honestly with the young people about sexuality, and small group involvement in conjunction with it is essential. It does provide visual involvement, however, which a pure lecture cannot do, and it offers the words of a highly talented, well-informed speaker. Our one caveat would be that it is no substitute for a living, sexual person, with whom adolescents might identify in a close, prolonged situation. Furthermore, it is our experience in working with extremely bright and/or sophisticated young people, that unless an audio-visual aid is unusually provocative, it can obstruct more than help.

Batten and McLean's program, *Fit to Be Tied*, is a different kind of presentation. It is dependent upon local talent—clergy, psychologists, physicians—and has a personal element that is lacking in Canon Green's presentation. There is much in the whole handbook that is good solid advice for developing this kind of program; for example: preinvolvement of parents; use of the film *Human Reproduction*; joint sessions with boys and girls; use of written questions, etc. But in all frankness, this course is heavy on sexual information and light on sexual attitudes. It is dated in that it really does not speak to the adolescent of 1970 (if it did to his counterpart in 1960). The very thing that is needed and should be expected from the Church, a theology of sex, is almost totally absent. The course depends heavily on the lecture-and-discussion technique, and no matter how "breezy" the style, we are not sure that the young people would listen.

Our greatest success in sex education with teenagers has been in a summer conference setting where clerical and lay leaders of attractive and certain sexuality "lived in" with the young people. There was only a minimum of talking *at* and a definite structure provided for talking *with* the youth, as well as countless informal opportunities. This is the best context for all that we can reasonably expect from adolescent sex education; namely, a clarification of sexual values and identity. It affords an opportunity for teenagers to relate to adults on a feeling level, not just on an intellectual plane, which can be followed up by some explication of the adult's understanding of the *meaning* of the sexual life.[49]

But I should emphasize that not even the "live-in" approach to adolescent sex education, when carried to its ultimate extreme (e.g., having an adolescent live in the home of a clergyman), will necessarily work miracles. I have seen cases where firm intellectual commitment to an ideal of masculinity, as well as real devotion to the adult ideal, ended in promiscuous behavior. Change does not always come easy.

IV. CONCLUSION

We are convinced that the Church must be in the business of sex education. Alden Hathaway has offered the interesting theory that one reason we ought to be there is that we have done so much in the last two thousand years to teach the wrong attitude toward sex.[50] He has a point, but we would go on to add that it is particularly important for us to be there because we must offer a theological basis for *the sexual person*. Once all appeals to expediency are exhausted —and there is nothing wrong in acting out of expediency —there will still remain the fact that the Church has the unique mission to proclaim the ultimate meaning of what it's all about.

* 7 *

A SUMMING UP

In summing up this report, it might be useful to frame certain general conclusions, agreed upon by all involved in the study, and to make some specific recommendations for parish programs. In doing this, there is a danger of appearing arrogant or presumptuous. But there is an equal risk in being so vague and so hesitant that the end result is little more than a list of platitudes. We want to avoid both extremes. To the best of our ability we have presented reliable data, a balanced view, and teaching that is true to the best traditions of the Church; and we hope that what we say in conclusion carries the same honesty to fact and devotion to truth.

First of all, we wish to emphasize the need for those responsible for the spiritual life of our congregations—the clergy, in most cases—to take seriously an understanding of the sexual person. Sexuality is a matter of great anxiety for people. It is not something peripheral to their prayer life, their family life, their hopes for Heaven, their sense of vocation, their role in society, or anything else that the average counselor may envision as his area of pastoral competence. It is something we must feel free to discuss as an appropriate concern.

I think we have to be very careful that in developing our own insights they do not become expressions of our personal anxieties and our efforts at reaching maturity. Moral decisions have to rest within an understanding of the person, and in this we need to weigh the contributions of our

113

Christian history as well as the insights learned from the behavioral and social sciences. In our use of this study we found that people wanted to know the physiological, psychological, and sociological facts. We must be able to provide these facts. But they particularly wanted to know what it all meant, which requires a theology as well. This makes our responsibility quite clear.

Second, when faced with Man's failing in sexual matters, we must take extreme care to avoid, at all costs, a judgmental attitude. Such an attitude can result only from a superficial understanding of the complex factors involved. It will not accomplish the desired reform; it will only intensify the guilt and alienation that the person already feels within himself.

We are not suggesting that sexual promiscuity (indiscriminate coitus, intercourse with more than one person) is other than a sin. At the same time, we would question an arbitrary labeling of masturbation as sinful. Generally, premarital coitus, and certainly extramarital relations, are a direct violation of God's intention for human sexuality. They *are* sinful. Human sexuality is potentially a very wonderful gift of God. It is an essential part of Man as God created him. Futhermore, the sin of its abuse is always a *social* sin, that is, it involves more than one person. It involves, of course, the partner in the act, but it also involves the sin of the parents, perhaps more than the sin of the individual. For the attitudes and feelings that are at the root of our sexual behavior are acquired more than anywhere else from our mother and father. Their failure in transmitting to us healthy attitudes and feelings are often first revealed in our destructive sexual behavior.

Much of the time, the attitude of the Church has been impossibly rigid and guilt-provoking, simply because it has viewed human sexuality in a non-Biblical, antisacramental, negative manner. For almost two thousand years our teaching has reflected the evolution of ideas rooted in the Greek horror of the irrational, particularly identified with a contempt for emotion and a fear of positive, sensual pleasure. This is undoubtedly a simplification, but it is generally true that people do not understand sex because, for one thing, the Church has failed to teach the creative role of human sexuality in God's plan in a positive, joyful manner.

In the third place, if blame must be placed for the abuse of human sexuality, we would place it upon the parents. The role of the Church is supportive; there is simply not the time, the opportunity, or the personnel necessary to enter into a continuing relationship with individuals where the limits and patterns of conduct can be held before them and effectively assimilated. This point is carefully expounded in chapter 2, on the psychological elements. Therefore, the Church's responsibility is *primarily* to the parents —the parents of children at all age levels.

It is not possible to begin sex education at the age of puberty, or later. Sex education begins at the time of conception. It is the acquired traits of the "inner man" that determine his ability to cope with the pressures of his own sexual drives and the conflicts of normal daily life. These traits are developed through the process of creative identification with parents and others over a long period of time; they are not something he gains through being "told." Tensions of society, the automobile, liquor, the communications media, etc., are only *secondary* factors in the sin of sexual promiscuity. To give them any more influence than this is to attempt, consciously or unconsciously, to escape our personal responsibility for the sexual behavior of our children. The whole matter must be handled, if it is to be done effectively, in the context of family life. We must see that the proper use of sex involves an insight into what it is to be a human being, and that we cannot grasp the nature of Man apart from the family relationship.

Finally, we are not impressed by reports of our current sophistication in matters of sexual knowledge. There is some evidence that with a growing sense of the value of the person among some of our more perceptive youth, there might be hope for a better understanding of sex's creative role in the next generation of adults, if those frightened people currently campaigning for a new "repressive society" are thwarted. But on the whole the open talk about sex is aimless and without purpose. Ignorance abounds, and as a result sex discussions are often either downright obscene or are patterned badinage characterized not only by mirth but by concealed anxiety and hostility toward the individuals being talked about. It would do the clerical raconteur, not to mention his lay brother, a great deal of good to examine Gershon Legman's very serious study of language, *The Rationale of the Dirty Joke*. There he would discover that it is not just the foul-mouthed young adolescent who is revealing the unhappy state of his unconscious life by his "open humor." [1] We must not settle for such an approach.

If the so-called sexual revolution is not going to be one more futile "swing of the pendulum," the Church must insist that in this new spirit of openness the parents assume the responsibility for a *sane* (not reacting irrationally out of their anxieties about themselves) and *informed* (realizing that to know that storks do not bring babies does not stimulate indiscriminate fornication) teaching of their children by example more than anything else. We are ready to admit that parents are often at a loss as to what they should teach by word and example because we, the Church, have failed to master the basic principles outlined in the paper on the theology of sex; we have failed to come to grips with the real questions, and consequently, we have failed to communicate reality of the subject to the parents. We, the Church, have to indicate *why* casual sexual behavior is destructive, and this can only be done if we know why it can be a profoundly creative element in human life.

What then may the parish priest do to address himself to this concern? There can be little doubt that he has a responsibility to do something!

The first specific recommendation grows out of our first general conclusion. Clergy and lay leaders need to read wisely in this field. The Bibliography lists some books we think are basic to a working knowledge of human sexuality, and we hope that the papers in this study will encourage the reader to explore the field for himself in greater detail and depth. One need not accept Freud totally to realize the vital role that man's sexual drive plays in so many areas of his life; areas to which the Church must speak. He simply cannot afford the luxury of ignorance, concepts unworthy of the Scriptures, or prejudice.

Second, the clergy or lay leader must recognize that the most effective means of ministering to people in this area is by entering into dialogue with small groups of parents at all age levels. He should see his role as supportive of their primary responsibility to speak to their children by word and, more important, by example. We would hope that he can feel comfortable in discussing with parents their real concerns about patterns of adolescent conduct, as there is obviously much anxiety in this area. As an objective, informed person he can be of great supportive assistance. He can draw them into programs of sex education that can be of great help in clarifying this whole area.

The clergyman might also see that his youth group advisers (who do not, by the very nature of their role, offer as much a threat in this area to their young people as does he) have an excellent opportunity to deal with the teen-ager in a realistic manner. It would be extremely helpful if he sought, therefore, to direct their discussion to some of the points made in the present study.

Third, if an adult assumes the role of a parent-surrogate —which he may in the physical or psychological absence of the parents—let him recognize from the start that he is a poor substitute. The chances are slim of his helping to-ward a successful resolution of the emotional conflicts and the sexual pressures that exhibit themselves in promiscuous behavior. He would probably be more effective by mak-ing sure that nothing in the life of the local parish implies permission for substandard sexual morality. The difficulty in chaperoning hayrides is reason enough to eliminate them. Dances involving children as young as 12 and 13, sponsored by the Church, are open for serious question. Late evening parties at someone's camp, with many dark corners and otherwise dimmed lights, only make a lie out of what we have perhaps elsewhere declared as the convictions of the Gospel.

Fourth, every pastor will or should have young people and not-so-young people come to him with problems of a direct or indirect sexual nature. The temptation is almost overpowering to trundle out the "Church's teaching" on this or that subject. The authoritative approach, reflected in this sort of imposition of arbitrary patterns of conduct, should be studiously avoided, not only in the pastor's study, but from the pulpit. There is great value here in client- or subject-centered counseling, where, by becoming a loving friend and permitting a person to reveal himself without fear of moral chastisement, we may find an opportunity to lead him to an understanding of appropriate sexual be-havior.

We do not mean here to give a "short course" in counseling, but simply to remind the reader of some of the basic fundamentals of a creative counseling relationship, so essential in this area of the pastoral ministry. Although we are more than ready to acknowledge that sexual promiscuity is a sin—both for the individual and for those responsible for his emotional maturity—we also acknowledge that much of what is done in irresponsible or casual sexual behavior is done in rebellion or in frustration. To assume a righteous pose not only aggravates the need to rebel and to adopt anti-social patterns, but is, in itself, immoral.

In closing, let us say that in the context of Man's working out the meaning of his sexuality there are marvelous opportunities for us to relate to him the meaning of the Gospel. This fact underlies our entire study. For while we have been concerned with a specific issue, we have been deeply aware of its far-reaching implications. We hope this study of human sexuality will be for all, as it has been for us, a way to a much more profound understanding of the ways of God with Man.

REFERENCE NOTES

FOREWORD

1. H. Kimball-Jones, *Toward a Christian Understanding of the Homosexual* (London: SCM, 1967), p. 95.

2. Peter and Barbara Wyden, *Growing Up Straight: What Every Thoughtful Parent Should Know About Homosexuality* (New York: Stein & Day, 1968). It has received some rather positive reviews. However, some reviewers dismiss it with the comment: "They . . . insist that it [homosexuality] is bad, bad, bad, and that if Dad will just play catch with junior it will vanish. . . . At no time do the authors mention that homosexuality is a kind of love . . . frequently involving love relationships of greater depth and maturity than many . . . among . . . heterosexuals." *Tangents*, Vol. 3, No. 1 (October, 1968), p. 8.

3. Martin Hoffman, *The Gay World: Male Homosexuality and the Social Creation of Evil* (New York: Basic Books, 1968); Stanley E. Willis, *Understanding and Counseling the Male Homosexual* (Boston: Little, Brown, 1967); Irving Bieber et al. *Homosexuality: A Psychoanalytic Study* (New York: Basic Books, 1962); Gore Vidal, *The City and the Pillar* (New York: New American Library, 1961); and Wainwright Churchill, *Homosexual Behavior Among Males* (New York: Hawthorn, 1967).

1. A THEOLOGY OF SEX

1. William Graham Cole, *Sex and Love in the Bible* (New York: Association, 1959), p. 300:
"Sex has another aim, another purpose, than procreation . . .

122 · The Sexual Person

sex as the creator of community is self-justifying and does not require procreation to justify it, or that the two ends are of equal status, and neither has claim to priority." (Notice that Cole uses the word "sex" in a narrow sense, as we use the word "coitus." Derrick Bailey's objection to this, as we subsequently present it in this chapter, is quite justified, we believe.) The official Roman Catholic view, however, is still that procreation is the primary purpose of sex. For example, read that arch-ultramontanist, Fr. Richard Ginder, "Right or Wrong," *Our Sunday Visitor*, Vol. 52, No. 36 (January 6, 1964), p. 2.

2. Derrick Sherwin Bailey, *The Man–Woman Relation in Christian Thought* (London: Longmans, 1959), p. 263.

3. Robert J. Stoller, *Sex and Gender: On the Development of Masculinity and Femininity* (New York: Science House, 1968), pp. 9–10.

4. Cole, *op. cit.*, p. 272.

5. Bailey, *op. cit.*, p. 265.

6. Karl Barth, *Church Dogmatics* (Edinburgh: T. & T. Clark, 1958), Vol. 3, Part 1, p. 186; cf., Tom F. Driver, "Sexuality and Jesus" Martin E. Marty and D. G. Peerman (eds.) *New Theology No. 3* (New York: Macmillan, 1966), p. 123, who refers to Barth's attitude regarding the relationship between human sexuality and the image of God.

7. Harvey G. Cox, *The Secular City: Secularization and Urbanization in Theological Perspective* (New York: Macmillan, 1964), pp. 192–216.

8. Nicolas Berdyaev, *The Destiny of Man* (trans.) Natalie Duddington (4th ed.; London: Geoffrey Bles, 1954), p. 53.

9. Our dependence here upon the works of Pierre Teilhard de Chardin, particularly *The Phenomenon of Man* (trans.) Bernard Wall (New York: Harper & Row, 1959), should be obvious to anyone who has read this great Jesuit.

10. Bailey, *op. cit.*, p. 273.

11. *Ibid.*, p. 278.

12. Carl Gustav Jung (eds.) Sir Herbert Read *et al. Collected Works* (trans.) R. F. C. Hull (New York: Pantheon, 1959), Vol. 9, Part 1, pp. 54 ff. and 290 ff.

13. Erich Fromm, *The Dogma of Christ and Other Essays on Religion, Psychology, and Culture* (New York: Holt, Rinehart & Winston, 1963), pp. 107–127.

14. Berdyaev, *op. cit.*, p. 62.

15. William Simon and John Gagnon, "Psychosexual Development," *Trans-action—Social Science and Modern Society*, Vol. 6, No. 5 (March 1969), pp. 15–16.

16. Cole, *op. cit.*, 273.

17. Edward Schillebeeckx, *Marriage: Secular Reality and Saving Mystery* (New York: Sheed & Ward, 1965), p. 17.

18. Fromm, *loc. cit.*

19. Derrick S. Bailey, *The Mystery of Love and Marriage: A Study in the Theology of Sexual Relation* (London: SCM, 1952), p. 44.

20. Otto A. Piper, *The Christian Interpretation of Sex* (New York: Scribner's, 1949), pp. 40–46.

21. *Ibid.*, p. 111.

22. Driver, *op. cit.* pp. 118–132.

23. *Ibid.*, p. 123. We cannot take too seriously the suggestion of Canon Hugh Montifiore that Jesus was homosexual. This most recent re-emergence of an old notion has no evidence to support it. See *The Living Church*, Vol. 155, No. 8 (August 20, 1967), p. 8.

24. Bailey, *Man–Woman, op. cit.*, p. 11.

25. Bernard Leeming, *Principles of Sacramental Theology* (London: Longmans, 1956), pp. 427 ff.

26. Bailey, *Mystery, op. cit.*, pp. 10–13, has an excellent brief summary of this theology.

27. Piper, *op. cit.*, pp. 55–56.

28. Barth, *op. cit.*, Vol. 3, Part 4, p. 134.

29. Bailey, *Mystery, op. cit.*, pp. 51–52; cf., Bailey, *Man-Woman, op. cit.*, pp. 9–10.

30. Piper, *op. cit.*, pp. 56 ff. Dr. Samuel Leavy makes a most helpful observation *from the psychoanalytic viewpoint* in regard to the whole discussion of the previous four paragraphs, when he writes: "Human sexual behavior is related to 'objects' [he does not use "objects" in the same sense we have]. That is,

it is not ordinarily, or for long periods, promiscuous, not a search for mere 'tension-reduction.' The sexual person is in search of another person, a 'thou' not an 'it,' with whom mutual understanding, love and concern are possible, although he may not always be aware of it, and although at times he may be seeming to be moving in the opposite direction from that which he professes. . . . Human beings want love, not only 'discharge,' which means that permanence has value in itself exceeding the value of conformity to divorce laws, or proprieties of the white middle class. Marriage, or something like it, is going to remain the preferred way to attain permanence, and it will do so because it corresponds to a human need."—Samuel A. Leavy, M.D., "Psychoanalysis and Moral Change," *Psychiatric Opinion*, Vol. 3, No. 5 (October, 1966), p. 36.

31. Piper, *op. cit.*, p. 63.

32. J. A. T. Robinson, *Liturgy Coming to Life* (2nd ed.; London: A. R. Mowbray, 1963), p. ix.

33. Ernest F. Bel (quoted from private correspondence). Leavy, *op. cit.*, p. 38, in support of what we and Fr. Bel suggest as possible, says that from the *clinical viewpoint* the evidence does not support the value of an *ironclad* transcendent absolute in matters of premarital sexuality. He says, "The question that is put in place of moral absolutes is more like this: does this kind of conduct make sense as a part of a whole life? Or, who is harmed or helped by it?"

34. Bernadine Kreis and Alice Pattie, *Up from Grief: Patterns of Recovery* (New York: Seabury, 1969), pp. 81, 83–84.

35. Morton M. Hunt, *The World of the Formerly Married* (New York: McGraw-Hill, 1966), p. 198. This is supported by a number of case studies.

36. Erik Erikson, *Young Man Luther: A Study in Psychoanalysis and History* (New York: Norton, 1958), p. 43.

37. Richard Rubenstein, *After Auschwitz: Radical Theology and Contemporary Judaism* (New York: Bobbs-Merrill, 1966), 269; cf. also, p. 273.

38. We are confident the reader may have turned his thoughts in this regard to the widely publicized (particularly

among the clergy) "Playboy Philosophy" of Hugh Hefner, editor of *Playboy* magazine. Undoubtedly many things Mr. Hefner protests about puritanical sexual codes are rightly questioned. But his alternatives for appropriate sexual behavior in our society are naive and superficial. Anyone interested in pursing contemporary critiques of the "Playboy Philosophy" might consult Richard F. Hettlinger *Living with Sex: The Student's Dilemma* (New York: Seabury, 1966), pp. 35–47; Rubenstein, *op. cit.*, pp. 267–287; and Cox, *loc. cit.* A further word might be said about Rubenstein's comments. They offer an explicit introduction to a refutation of the theory that *sex is play*, and that because religion adopts a solemn attitude toward it, it is necessarily imparting to it a sense of guilt. Perhaps the most radical exponent of the "sex is play" notion, and the most explicit antagonist to the position of this study, is Maurice Parmelee in *The Play Function of Sex* (New York: Vantage, 1966).

39. Lester A. Kirkendall, *Premarital Intercourse and Interpersonal Relations* (New York: Julian, 1961), pp. 199–200.

40. Cf. Vincent Taylor, *The Gospel According to St. Mark: The Greek Text with Introduction Notes and Indexes* (London: Macmillan & Co., Ltd., 1952), p. 421. Edward B. Guerry, *The Historic Principle of the Indissolubility of Marriage* (Sewanee: The University Press, 1953), p. 50ff., as well as the entire book, offers some helpful material on this subject.

41. Piper, *op. cit.*, p. 161.

42. Bailey, *Mystery, op. cit.*, pp. 70–96.

43. Leeming, *op. cit.*, p. 279; also see *Doctrine in the Church of England* (London: S.P.C.K., 1952), p. 201: "Further we desire to affirm that in the case of two *Christian* persons freely undertaking before God to enter on a lifelong marriage union, *grace is afforded* which, if reliance is fully placed upon it, will enable the persons concerned to fulfil the obligations involved and to rise to the opportunities offered in their married life in spite of all difficulties however grave." (Italics ours.)

44. Leeming, *op. cit.*, p. 275.

45. *Ibid.*, p. 271.
46. Massey H. Shepherd, Jr., *The Oxford American Prayer Book Commentary* (New York: Oxford U.P. 1950), p. 300.
47. L. Duchesne, *Christian Worship*, p. 428, *cit.* William Kemp Lowther Clark and Charles Harris (eds.), *Liturgy and Worship: A Companion to the Prayer Books of the Anglican Communion* (London: S.P.C.K., 1932), p. 461.
48. Bruno Bettelheim, *The Children of the Dream* (New York: Macmillan, 1969), outlines the role of the Israeli kibbutz as a generally successful socialization surrogate for the family.
49. Bailey, *Man–Woman, op. cit.*, p. 98.

2. PSYCHOLOGICAL FACTORS IN CURRENT SEXUAL BEHAVIOR

1. The reader should note that the point of view concerning a "sexual revolution" in this chapter differs radically from that in the chapter that follows, "A Sociology of the Sexual Morality of Youth." This accurately portrays the division of opinion that often exists between psychiatry and sociology. The point of view expressed in this chapter (4), whereas argued often *ad hominem*, is not that of Dr. Olivier alone. In our recent conversation with the chairman of graduate studies in the Department of Psychiatry at Marquette University, Dr. Basil Jackson (who also specializes in the treatment of children and adolescents), he stated that beyond doubt there is a notable relaxing of superego limits in regard to overt sexual behavior. The reply of the sociologist to that claim can be found in the discussion of Dr. Graham B. Blaine's opinion on page 44.
2. Brittain M. Moore, "The Epidermiology of Syphilis," *Journal of the American Medical Association*, Vol. 186, No. 9 (November 1963), p. 831.
3. From 1940 to 1965 absolute increase is over 300% (7.1 per 1000 unmarried women to 23.5 per 1000 unmarried women). *The World Almanac: 1969 Edition* (New York: Newspaper Enterprise Assoc. Inc., 1969), p. 764.

4. Ernest Jones, "The Origin of the Superego," *International Journal of Psychoanalysis*, 1926.

5. Erik H. Erikson, "The Problem of Ego Identity," *Journal of the American Psychoanalytic Association*, Vol. 4, No. 1 (1956).

6. S. Ferenczi, "Psychoanalysis of Sexual Habits, *International Journal of Psycho-analysis*, Vol. 6, Part 4 (October 1925), p. 380.

3. A SOCIOLOGY OF THE SEXUAL
MORALITY OF YOUTH

1. Alfred C. Kinsey *et al.*, *Sexual Behavior in the Human Male* (Philadelphia: Saunders, 1948).

2. *Ibid.*, p. 395.

3. *Ibid.*, p. 396.

4. *Ibid.*, p. 407.

5. *Ibid.*, pp. 396–397.

6. *Ibid.*, p. 397.

7. Cf. William Graham Sumner, *Folkways: A Study of the Sociological Importance of Usages, Manners, Customs, Mores, and Morals* (Boston: Ginn & Co., 1906).

8. Alfred C. Kinsey *et al.*, *Sexual Behavior in the Human Female* (Philadelphia: Saunders, 1953). The top two rows of data come from Table 65, p. 275; the third and fourth rows come from Table 83, p. 339. The size of the sample was about 3900 women.

9. *Ibid.*, p. 299.

10. Erwin O. Smigel and Rita Seiden, "The Decline and Fall of the Double Standard," *The Annals of the American Academy of Political and Social Science*, Vol. 376 (March 1968), pp. 7, 12. This point of view—that only attitude, not sexual behavior, has changed markedly since Kinsey—is supported by a survey by Ira E. Robinson *et al.*, "Change in Sexual Behavior and Attitudes of College Students," *The Family Coordinator*, Vol. 17, No. 2 (April 1968), pp. 119–123.

11. Ira Reiss, *The Social Context of Premarital Sexual Per-*

missiveness (New York: Holt, Rinehart & Winston, 1967), p. 233.

12. Kinsey, *Human Male, op. cit.*, p. 330.

13. Kinsey, *Human Female, op. cit.*, p. 336.

14. Ira Reiss, *Social Problems*, Vol. 4 (April 1957), p. 334.

15. Winston Ehrmann, *Journal of the National Association of Women Deans and Counsellors*, Vol. 26 (January 1963), pp. 25–26.

16. *Ibid.*

17. Vance Packard, *Sexual Wilderness* (New York: McKay, 1968), pp. 185–186.

18. Ehrmann, *op. cit.*, p. 24.

19. Warren Breed, "Sex, Class and Socialization in Dating," *Marriage and Family Living*, Vol. 18 (May 1956), pp. 137–144.

20. Mervin B. Freedman, "The Sexual Behavior of American College Women: An Empirical Study and an Historical Survey" (a yet unpublished paper made available to Dr. Breed). Similar material appears in Mervin B. Freedman, *The College Experience* (San Francisco: Jossey-Bass, 1967), pp. 81–105.

21. *Ibid.*

22. See, for example, books by Frederick Wertham, a New York psychiatrist.

23. Cf. Bibliography in Joseph Klapper, *The Effects of Mass Communication* (New York: Free Press, 1960), chap. 6.

24. Smigel and Seiden, *op. cit.*, pp. 10–11.

25. Floyd Mansfield Martinson, *Marriage and the American Ideal* (New York: Dodd, Mead, 1960), pp. 215–219.

26. Seymour Morgan Farber and Roger H. L. Wilson, *Teen-Age Marriage and Divorce: A Symposium* (San Francisco: Diablo, 1967), p. 1. "At the present time 40 per cent of all brides are between the ages of 15 and 18. Half of these marriages break up within five years. In fact, it has been estimated that the divorce rate among those who marry before the age of 18 is two to four times as high as among those who marry later."

27. Breed, *op. cit.*

28. Martinson, *op. cit.*, chap. 14.

29. The works of Margaret Mead, Talcott Parson, and almost any sociology text.

30. Kenneth Keniston, *The Young Radicals: Notes on Committed Youth* (New York: Harcourt, Brace & World, 1968), p. 281; Michael Novak, *A Theology of Radical Politics* (New York: Herder & Herder, 1969), pp. 103–108.

31. Freedman, *op. cit.*, thinks of most college students as unsophisticated, disinterested, and emotionally stable.

4. Mass Communication Media and Morality

1. Gerhart Saenger, "Male and Female Relations in the American Comic Strip," *Public Opinion Quarterly,* Vol. 19, pp. 194–205.

2. Frederick Elkin, "The Psychological Appeal of the Hollywood Western," *Journal of Educational Sociology*, Vol. 24, pp. 72–86.

3. Rudolf Arnheim, "The World of the Daytime Serial," in Paul Felix Lazarsfeld and F. N. Stanton (eds.), *Radio Research, 1942–1943* (Toronto: Collins, 1944).

4. W. L. Warner and W. E. Henry, "The Radio Daytime Serial," *Genetic Psychology Monographs*, Vol. 37, pp. 3–71.

5. Herta Herzog, "What Do We Really Know About Daytime Serial Listeners," Lazarsfeld and Stanton, *op. cit.*

6. Warren Breed, "Some Content Themes in TV Family Dramas" (unpublished paper).

7. Norman Podhoretz, "Our Changing Ideals, as Seen on TV," *Commentary*, Vol. 17 (1954), pp. 534–540.

8. *Newsweek*, Vol. 73 (Feb. 24, 1969), p. 101.

9. S. H. Lovibond, "Effect of Media Stressing Crime and Violence Upon Children's Attitudes," *Social Problems*, Vol. 15, No. 1 (Summer 1967), p. 91.

10. Frederick C. Wertham, *Seduction of the Innocent* (New York: Rinehart, 1954).

11. Harry J. Skornia, *Television and Society: An Inquest and Agenda for Improvement* (New York: McGraw-Hill, 1965), pp. 143–144.

12. *Ibid.*, p. 144.

13. *Ibid.*, pp. 150–156.

14. *Ibid.*, p. 174.

15. Joseph T. Klapper, *The Effects of Mass Communication* (New York: Free Press, 1960).

16. Kyle Haselden, *Morality and the Mass Media* (Nashville: Broadman, 1968), pp. 73 ff.

17. Edward A. Ricutti, "Children and Radio," *Genetic Psychology Monographs*, Vol. 44, pp. 69–143.

18. Herbert S. Lewin, "Facts and Fears About the Comics," *Nation's Schools*, Vol. 52, pp. 46–48.

19. Hilde Therese Himmelweit *et al.*, *Television and the Child: An Empirical Study of the Effect of Television on the Young* (Oxford: U.P., 1958).

20. Katherine Wolf and Marjorie Fiske, "The Children Talk About Comics," in Paul Felix Lazarsfeld and F. N. Stanton (eds.), *Communications Research 1948–1949* (Toronto: Musson; New York: Harper, 1949).

21. Lovibond, *op. cit.*, p. 98.

22. *Ibid.*

23. Walter M. Gerson, "Mass Media Socialization Behavior: Negro–White Differences," *Social Forces*, Vol. 45, No. 1 (1966), pp. 40–50.

24. Haddon W. Robinson, "The Impact of Religious Radio and Television Programs in American Life," *Bibliotheca Sacra*, Vol. 123 (1966), pp. 124–135.

25. "Problèmes psychologiques en matière d'education sanitaire et d'information mèdicale," *Annales Mèdico-Psychologiques*, Vol. 1 (1967), Part 1, p. 297.

26. Eleanor E. Maccoby, "Why Do Children Watch TV?" *Public Opinion Quarterly*, Vol. 18, pp. 142–156.

27. *Time*, Vol. 84, No. 15 (Nov. 6, 1964), p. 76.

28. Reported in Ira Oscar Glick and Sidney J. Levy, *Living With Television* (Chicago: Aldine, 1962), p. 75.

29. Gary Albert Steiner, *The People Look at Television: A Study of Audience Attitudes* (New York: Knopf, 1963), pp. 83–91.

30. Dallas Smythe, "Reality as Presented by Television," *Public Opinion Quarterly*, Vol. 18, pp. 142–156.

31. Seward Hiltner and Karl Menninger (eds.), *Constructive Aspects of Anxiety* (New York: Abingdon, 1963), pp. 71, 127; Rollo May, *The Meaning of Anxiety* (New York: Ronald, 1950), pp. 102–112; Thomas W. Klink, *Depth Perspectives in Pastoral Work* (Englewood Cliffs, N.J.: Prentice-Hall, 1965), p. 42, reminds us that "learning doth make a bloody entrance."

32. Louis E. Raths *et al.*, *Values and Teaching: Working with Values in the Classroom* (Columbus, Ohio: C. E. Merrill, 1966), pp. 15 ff.

33. John Wilson *et al.*, *Introduction to Moral Education* (Baltimore: Penguin, 1967), pp. 349–360.

34. Kenneth Keniston, *The Young Radicals* (New York: Harcourt, Brace & World, 1968), pp. 60–67.

35. Haselden, *op. cit.*, p. 93.

36. *Ibid.*, pp. 94–96.

5. MASTURBATION

1. William Howell Masters and Virginia E. Johnson, *Human Sexual Response* (Boston: Little, Brown, 1966), p. 197.

2. Richard F. Hettlinger, *Living with Sex: The Student's Dilemma* (New York: Seabury, 1966), p. 144.

3. Alfred C. Kinsey *et al.*, *Sexual Behavior in the Human Male* (Philadelphia: Saunders, 1948), p. 499.

4. Masters and Johnson, *loc. cit.*

5. George Hagmaier and Robert W. Gleason, *Counseling the Catholic: Modern Techniques and Emotional Conflicts* (New York: Sheed & Ward, 1959), p. 215. Derrick Sherwin Bailey, *The Man–Woman Relation in Christian Thought* (London: Longmans, 1959), pp. 160–161, discusses the view of St. Thomas Aquinas.

6. Robert Cecil Mortimer, *The Elements of Moral Theology* (London: Adam and Charles Black, 1947), pp. 182–183.

7. Masters and Johnson, *op. cit.*, 201–202. All admitted to masturbation, but none to "excessive masturbation."

8. Mortimer, *op. cit.*, p. 181.

9. *Ibid.*, p. 180.

10. *Ibid.*, p. 179.

11. Hettlinger, *op. cit.*, p. 87.

12. Glanville Llewelyn Williams, *The Sanctity of Life and the Criminal Law* (New York: Knopf, 1957), pp. 138–41.

13. *Ibid.*, p. 139.

14. *Ibid.*, p. 49.

15. William Graham Cole, *Sex and Love in the Bible* (New York: Association, 1960), p. 363. "The Eastern Orthodox Churches extend the use of the latter term [μαλακοί] to all those who procure orgasm or sexual pleasure in ways other than normal intercourse, but this is an extreme which goes beyond both the Greek of the New Testament and classical Greek."

16. Williams, *op. cit.*, pp. 136–137; Gerhard von Rad, *Genesis* (Philadelphia: Westminster, 1961), p. 353; Samuel Rolles Driver, *The Book of Genesis* (3rd ed.; New York: Gorham, 1905), p. 328. But see also Cole, *op. cit.*, p. 297, who leaves the question open as to whether or not Onan practiced masturbation. He does point out, however, that the "sin" was his failure to fulfill the levirate obligation.

17. Hagmaier and Gleason, *op. cit.*, pp. 74–75.

18. *Ibid.*, p. 76.

19. James Kavanaugh, *A Modern Priest Looks at His Outdated Church* (New York: Simon & Schuster [Trident], 1967), p. 185.

20. Robert P. O'Neil and Michael A. Donovan, *Sexuality and Moral Responsibility* (Washington: Corpus Books, 1968), pp. 107–108.

21. Herbert Waddams, *A New Introduction to Moral Theology* (New York: Seabury, 1965), p. 143.

22. Helmut Thielicke, *The Ethics of Sex* (trans.) John W. Doberstein (New York: Harper & Row, 1964), p. 255.

23. *Ibid.*, p. 256.

24. Walter Stokes in the *Medical Tribune*, February 21, 1964.

25. Oliver Spurgeon English and Gerald H. J. Pearson, *Emotional Problems of Living: Avoiding the Neurotic Pattern* (rev. ed., New York: Norton, 1955), pp. 82, 85.

26. *Sex and the College Student: A Developmental Perspective on Sexual Issues on the Campus* (New York: Group for the Advancement of Psychiatry, 1965), p. 71.

27. Rhoda L. Lorand, *Love, Sex and the Teenager* (New York: Macmillan, 1965), p. 63.

28. Masters and Johnson, *op. cit.*, p. 202.

29. Hagmaier and Gleason, *op. cit.*, pp. 78, 79.

30. Lorand, *op. cit.*, p. 63. Cf. William Hulme, *Youth Considers Sex* (New York: Nelson, 1965), pp. 41 ff., who bases his attack on masturbation on its inwardness and openness to fantasy, and who fails to take into account this positive and perhaps necessary element in human development. Can we fulfill an overt relationship until it has become a living possibility in our own mind? It is surprising that someone as sophisticated as Hulme in pastoral psychology seems to offer such a superficial critique of masturbation.

31. Lorand, *op. cit.*, pp. 66–67.

32. Hagmaier and Gleason, *op. cit.*, p. 88. This is a valid qualification, as Lorand, *op. cit.*, pp. 66–67, states.

33. William Stringfellow, *Instead of Death* (New York: Seabury, 1963), p. 34. Cf. Richard L. Rubenstein, *After Auschwitz: Radical Theology and Contemporary Judaism* (New York: Bobbs-Merrill, 1966), p. 275.

34. Lorand, *op. cit.*, pp. 66–68.

35. Hettlinger, *op. cit.*, p. 92.

6. Sex Education and the Church

1. *Time*, Vol. 89, No. 23 (June 9, 1967), pp. 36–37.

2. A brief history of the campaign was issued in the spring of 1969 in a memorandum from the national headquarters of Planned Parenthood to its member agencies. It is from this that the judgment here is drawn.

3. "The real sex education of the child actually begins at

birth, for the way the child is held by the mother and father, his association of the feel of their muscles, the touch of their skin, their characteristic body odor, and the sounds of their voices with their maleness and femaleness, his association with what their voices are expressing to and about each other and to and about him with maleness and femaleness—love, hate, cruelty, indifference, rejection—this is powerful sex education with enormous import for sexual conditioning."—Mary S. Calderone, in an article, "The Development of Healthy Sexuality," distributed by the American Association for Health, Physical Education, and Recreation, a department of the National Education Association.

4. John H. Gagnon, "Sexuality and Sexual Learning in the Child," *Psychiatry*, Vol. 28, No. 3 (August 1965), p. 223.

5. *Ibid.*

6. Calderone, *op. cit.*

7. From personal conversations with Chaplain Charles Goldsmith.

8. Leslie H. Farber, "I'm Sorry Dear," in Edward and Ruth Brecher (eds.), *An Analysis of Human Sexual Response* (Boston: Little, Brown, 1966), pp. 291–311.

9. *Milwaukee Journal*, May 15, 1969, Part 1, p. 15.

10. Leon Salzman, *The Obsessive Personality: Origins, Dynamics, and Therapy* (New York: Science House, 1968), pp. 72–85, gives an insight into this kind of person—the scrupulous, obsessive-compulsive, "up tight" individual—who has an overwhelming need to control all elements of sexuality and is faced with real panic when his control is threatened. Since these persons are often very "religious," we think it is important for clergy and lay leaders to understand this type.

11. *Milwaukee Journal*, May 18, 1969, Part 5, p. 5; Harold Prince predicts the return of "Victorianism," and we may be just sick enough for it to happen.

12. Calderone, *op. cit.*

13. *Cit.* Gagnon, *op. cit.*, p. 223.

14. Carl Gustav Jung (eds.) Sir Herbert Read *et al. Collected Works* (New York: Pantheon, 1954), Vol. 17, pp. 32–33.

15. Gerald Caplan and Serge Lebovici (eds.), *Adolescence: Psychosocial Perspectives* (New York: Basic Books, 1969), pp. 105–112; see also, chapter 2 of this study.

16. Gertrude B. Couch, "Youth Looks at Sex," *Adolescence*, Vol. 5, No. 6 (Summer 1967), p. 260. (Italics added.)

17. From a list of 114 written questions asked by seventh-grade boys and girls in a sex education program at Oconomowoc Junior High, Oconomowoc, Wis.

18. Frank Furstenberg *et al.*, "Birth Control Knowledge and Attitudes Among Unmarried Pregnant Adolescents: A Preliminary Report," *Journal of Marriage and the Family*, Vol. 31, No. 1 (February 1969), p. 42.

19. Erik H. Erikson, *Identity: Youth and Crisis* (New York: Norton, 1968), p. 136.

20. Caplan and Lebovici, *op. cit.*, p. 15.

21. *Ibid.*, p. 106.

22. John Wilson *et al.*, *Introduction to Moral Education* (Baltimore: Penguin, 1967), p. 307.

23. *Ibid.*, pp. 400–403.

24. *National Catholic Reporter*, Vol. 5, No. 26 (April 23, 1969), p. 9.

25. In Mark J. Link (ed.), *Teaching the Sacraments and Morality* (Chicago: Loyola U.P., 1965), p. 189.

26. In Seymour Morgan Faber and Roger H. L. Wilson (eds.), *Sex Education and the Teenager: A Symposium* (San Francisco: Diablo, 1967), p. 32.

27. A resolution of the Association for Health, Physical Education, and Recreation, in March 1966, regarding sex education suggests that the Church can be a helpful instrument in getting schools to initiate programs in sex education.

28. "Sex education of the young begins with sex education of the adults." Alden M. Hathaway, "Sex Education in the Church," *Pastoral Psychology*, Vol. 19, No. 184 (May 1968), p. 8.

29. Robert Farrar Capon, *Bed and Board* (New York: Simon & Schuster, 1965), p. 49.

30. Hathaway, *op. cit.*, pp. 9–10.

31. Calderone, *op. cit.:* "The schools will have to assume

the main burden and responsibility for planning and carrying out adequate sex education programs, with the churches backing them up by developing the moral concepts about human relationships including sex."

32. Earl Herbert Brill, *Sex Is Dead and Other Postmortems* (New York: Seabury, 1967), p. 13.

33. As a beginning in this area we would recommend Reuel L. Howe, *The Miracle of Dialogue* (New York: Seabury, 1963); John L. Casteel (ed.), *The Creative Role of Interpersonal Groups in the Church Today* (New York: Association, 1968); and Clyde Reid, *Groups Alive—Church Alive* (New York: Harper & Row, 1969). Someone who wishes to do more advanced reading might start with a basic work of the pioneers in this field: Warren Bennis *et al.*, *Interpersonal Dynamics: Essays and Readings on Human Interaction* (rev. ed.; Homewood, Ill.: Dorsey, 1968). To anyone who particularly wishes to relate the use of audio-visual materials—referred to on several occasions in this study—we recommend John Harrell, *Teaching Is Communicating: An Audio-Visual Handbook for Church Use* (New York: Seabury, 1965).

34. The literature in the field of premarital counseling is not what we might wish. Russell L. Dicks, *Premarital Guidance* (Englewood Cliffs, N.J.: Prentice-Hall, 1963), is the pertinent volume in the "Successful Pastoral Counseling Series," and it suffers many of the problems shared by that series as a whole. The late Dr. Dicks, a pioneer in the field of pastoral counseling, maintains a point of view somewhat in contradiction with that expressed in our study. The book itself is designed more as a study guide for premarital *groups*. Aaron L. Rutledge, *Premarital Counseling* (Cambridge, Mass.: Schenkman, 1966), offers a comprehensive study of this field by a secular marriage counselor. Clergy could profit greatly from reading this. Wayne E. Oates, *Premarital Pastoral Care and Counseling* (Nashville: Broadman, 1958), is a very brief guide by the eminent Baptist pastoral theologian, designed for clergy of his own denomination. It is not one of his more notable works and is of limited use. James Kenneth Morris, *Premarital*

Counseling: A Manual for Ministers (Englewood Cliffs, N.J.: Prentice-Hall, 1960), is now out of print and not available to us.

35. Two books on marital counseling *per se* should be familiar to every clergyman. Begin with Charles William Stewart, *The Minister as Marriage Counselor* (New York: Abingdon, 1961). This book will at some point, perhaps immediately, strike the reader as too superficial. When it does, move on to Virginia Satir, *Conjoint Family Therapy: A Guide to Theory and Technique* (rev. ed.; Palo Alto, Calif.: Science and Behavior Books, 1967). It is difficult reading, but worth the effort.

36. The Episcopal canon says that only one party must be baptized. This seems to make little sense to us, since both must take Christian vows, and it would appear immoral to ask a non-Christian to do so. Perhaps the argument is based on the Pauline contention that the Christian spouse sanctifies the pagan.

37. Perhaps this question alarms the pseudopropriety of some clergy. We have never had the prospective bride answer anything but "yes" or "no" (and in one case, "We can't agree —the doctor and I!"), and take it as a perfectly normal question. If a priest feels unbearably uncomfortable with this kind of a question, he needs to ask himself what it means to be a pastor in relation to the lives of his people and what his feelings are about his own sexuality. The point of the question is that you must determine if coercion is present, and this would be the commonest form. The answer will be "yes" about two out of five times. It does not mean you should not marry them; but it does mean that you must explore their reasons much more deeply than otherwise.

38. These concepts are treated in the present volume; material for further study is suggested in the Bibliography.

39. People wishing to explore further the rationale behind the "encounter" technique might read the works of O. Hobart Mowrer, in particular a large volume edited by him, *Morality and Mental Health* (Chicago: Rand McNally, 1967); William

Glasser, *Reality Therapy: A New Approach to Psychiatry* (New York: Harper & Row, 1965); John W. Drakeford, *Integrity Therapy* (Nashville: Broadman, 1967); William Carl Schutz, *Joy: Expanding Human Awareness* (New York: Grove, 1967); and Frederick C. Wood, Jr., "Pre-Marital Counseling: A Mild Polemic and a Modest Proposal," *Pastoral Psychology*, Vol. 20, No. 197 (October 1969). We are still awaiting a definitive work on so-called provocative therapy in terms of pastoral counseling—which is the next step from the approach essentially outlined in these works and which is being tried throughout the country.

40. This is what W. Clark Ellzey calls the "teachable moment" in marriage. "Education for the Newly Married," *Pastoral Psychology*, Vol. 19, No. 184 (May 1968), p. 21. This article as well as Thomas C. McGinnis, *Your First Year of Marriage* (New York: Doubleday, 1967), provide good background reading for this program.

41. It is for this approach that William Gennè pleads in "The Educational Context of Marriage Counseling," *Pastoral Psychology*, Vol. 19, No. 184 (May 1968), pp. 5–6.

42. Lester A. Kirkendall, review of Richard Ayers and Charles Tooman, *Young Adult Enrichment Program: Sex Education*, in *The Family Coordinator*, Vol. 17, No. 2 (April, 1968), p. 134.

43. Whereas we are rather critical of the *Marriage Enrichment Program*, it is only fair to say that not everyone shares our opinion. William A. Dalgish *et al.* (eds.), *Media for Christian Formation: A Guide to Audio-Visual Resources* (Dayton, Ohio: Pflaum, 1969), pp. 185–186, describes it as "straightforward and reverent . . . both comprehensive and scientifically accurate."

44. Herbert A. Otto, *Group Methods Designed to Actualize Human Potentials (A handbook)*.

45. We are grateful to the Rev. Peter Stone, rector of St. Matthew's Episcopal Church, Kenosha, Wis., for his description of this program.

46. A good place to read about this would be Schutz, *op. cit.*
47. Otto, *op. cit.*, p. 52.
48. *Ibid.*, p. 56.
49. If our intention here is hopelessly obscure, we recommend reading Charles A. Curran, *Counseling and Psychotherapy* (New York: Sheed & Ward, 1968), pp. 74 ff.
50. Hathaway, *op. cit.*, p. 7.

7. A SUMMING UP

1. Gershon Legman, *The Rationale of the Dirty Joke: An Analysis of Sexual Humor* (New York: Grove, 1968).

A SELECT ANNOTATED BIBLIOGRAPHY

It is beyond the scope of this study to furnish a complete bibliography of the multitude of books published on sex education. What is offered here, therefore, is a list of books that we judge will be helpful to clergy, lay leaders, and concerned adults, without any suggestion that these are the only ones of value. It can best be said that these are the ones that have been brought to our attention, that we have examined, and that we recommend to you.

For anyone wishing to keep abreast of the field, we recommend two things: First, that he get his name and address on the mailing list of Family Life Publications, Inc., P.O. Box 6725, Durham, N.C., 27708. Not only do these people publish the SKI (see page 98) and related tests (as well as a new *Drug Knowledge Inventory*), but they also provide a list of books of interest to the marriage and family counselor. Second, that he subscribe to *SIECUS Newsletter* (cost: $2.00 a year), the publication of the Sex Education and Information Council of the United States, 1855 Broadway, New York, N.Y., 10023. This provides, along with excellent articles, first-rate evaluations of material in the field.

Books for the Clergy and Lay Leaders

Listed here are books of more than general interest, which will provide the basis of an informed ministry for the priest or lay leader engaged in sex, marriage, and family counseling and education. These are in addition to the books listed in subsequent sections of this Bibliography, which he should also have read or be familiar with.

BAILEY, DERRICK SHERWIN. *The Mystery of Love and Marriage: A Study in the Theology of Sexual Relation* (New York: Harper & Row, 1952). O.p.*
This is a superb theological study of great value to anyone who seeks a sound background for his own thinking and counseling. It is a seminal work in this study. It makes much use of such theologians as Martin Buber and does not subscribe to a very rigid line in matters such as marital indissolubility.

———. *Sexual Relation in Christian Thought* (New York: Harper & Row, 1959). O.p.
Again, this is a basic work. The most complete historical survey recently published, its frank appraisal of our past misconceptions in this area does much to force us to examine honestly our own attitudes. If you are interested in what the Church Fathers, such as Augustine, taught, or in what transpired during the Reformation, here is your source. It concludes with an excellent chapter: "Towards a Theology of Sex."

BELL, ROBERT R. *Premarital Sex in a Changing Society* (Englewood Cliffs, N.J.: Prentice-Hall, 1966).
A very helpful sociological study, which supports the position of chapter 3 in this book. It is most readable and provides an analysis of all sociological evaluations to the date of publication.

BERTOCCI, PETER A. *Sex, Love and the Person* (New York: Sheed & Ward, 1967).
A closely reasoned exposition by an eminent philosopher of

* Books marked "O.p." are out-of-print with the publisher, but may be available at local libraries or secondhand bookstores.

the need to confine petting and intercourse to marriage, because they are intimately involved in the question of value and its contribution to the growth of the person. He says many of the same things that chapter 1, "A Theology of Sex," says, with perhaps a greater desire to maintain an absolute consistency to his position. It is not easy reading, but worth the effort for someone seeking a basis for a relatively conservative position founded upon the now popular theology of the person. We recommend it highly.

BLANCK, RUBIN and GERTRUDE. *Marriage and Personal Development* (New York: Columbia U.P., 1968).

This is a simple, readable introduction to the psychology of marriage from the psychoanalytical view (which would be different, but not incompatible to what Satir [see below] writes). Ego psychology, such as is found in Theodore Lidz's analysis (see below), underlies the assumption here that marriage is a step in human development. "Ego function is rooted in the framework of a dyadic relationship, in which optimal growth takes place under conditions whereby maturational and developmental processes are synchronized in an environment which includes the libidinal availability of another person." If you begin to understand that statement and the approach appeals to you, you will find this book helpful. It has been very well reviewed by psychoanalytical colleagues of the Blancks.

BRECHER, EDWARD and RUTH (eds.). *An Analysis of Human Sexual Response* (Boston: Little, Brown, 1966).

This book does just what the title suggests; analyzes some of the questions raised by the Masters and Johnson study. These include such questions as the source and kind of subjects for the study, methods used in the study, sex problems in marriage counseling, methods of overcoming frigidity, etc. It is most fascinating and informative, if somewhat clinical, and it saves the necessity of laboring over the Masters and Johnson report itself.

BROWN, THOMAS E. *A Guide for Christian Sex Education of Youth* (New York: Association, 1968).

If you are planning sex education in a parish or interparochial setting on the three- or four-session model, this is a must. It is hard to conceive of a more thorough, careful guide to setting up this kind of program. Mr. Brown is a cautious informant, well versed in his subject and concerned to promote more or less traditional Christian morality. In chapter 6 we state our reservations about even the best of this kind of adolescent sex education.

BUYTENDIJK, F. J. J. *Woman: A Contemporary View*. Trans. DENIS J. BARRETT (New York: Association, 1968).

Buytendijk is a Dutch psychologist, whom Abel Jeanniere (see Appendix to chapter 1) all too lightly dismisses, but whom we believe gives the most objective and realistic appraisal of modern woman we know. Like Jeanniere, he is a phenomenologist; but unlike Jeanniere and all too many of that school, he takes hormones and genitals seriously. He believes that woman is different from man and there is such a thing as femininity. We recommend this as a solid study in accord with our own convictions.

FRIEDENBERG, EDGAR Z. *The Vanishing Adolescent* (New York: Dell, 1962).

This author is of great importance, even though the book itself in its original form is over ten years old. Friedenberg's thesis is that by demanding an early patterning and conformity to adult standards and values, we are losing the essential function of adolescence and hence destroying the creativity of our society. This has obvious implications for sexuality. He should be read in conjunction with Kenneth Keniston (see below), who describes the "new adolescent" who has broken out of this pattern. However, we suspect that Friedenberg's teenager is still in the majority.

GROUP FOR THE ADVANCEMENT OF PSYCHIATRY. *Sex and the College Student.* (2nd ed.; New York: Fawcett World, 1967).

An extremely interesting study, it supports the role of the university or college *in loco parentis.* It argues this from clinical data, arriving at a point of view calling for a perceptive use of external discipline, a position not uncommon among members of the psychiatric profession these days (whom we have even heard accused of being excessively "moralistic"). College chaplains—particularly those supporting "open dorms" and the like—will find this study a little sobering, whether they agree or not.

HODGSON, LEONARD. *Sex and Christian Freedom: An Enquiry* (New York: Seabury, 1967).

The author describes this as an inquiry rather than an exposition, which is indicative of his purpose to explore Biblical insights and to avoid absolute judgments on every given act of sexuality. "What we have to do is try to listen with understanding sympathy to what we are told (by those who come to us) and be prepared to start with each person *at the point which he or she has reached* in the order of learning." This is a book that has a position to state that is more permissive than that of Peter Bertocci, but is also based on a theology of the person.

KENISTON, KENNETH. *The Young Radicals: Notes on Committed Youth* (New York: Harcourt, Brace & World, 1968).

Movements change so rapidly that one is hesitant in saying that this is *the* analysis of contemporary youth. For one thing, it analyzes only the "new left," the activist group of young people out to change our society. For another, it is written by a social psychologist from his particular point of view (Friedenberg, whom we have already recommended, is a sociologist and educator). But with this in mind, it should be read along with Friedenberg to understand contemporary youth culture.

KIRKENDALL, LESTER A. *Premarital Intercourse and Interpersonal Relationships* (New York: Julian, 1961).

In theory, a "dull sociological study." In fact, this is an exciting book which required a second printing in 1965 and has been widely distributed by the Pastoral Psychology Book Club. It is as significant a writing as anyone counseling in the field of sex and marriage might read. Many theological insights are supported by sociological evidence. It is not, however, a book for the prudish.

LIDZ, THEODORE. *The Person: His Development Throughout the Life Cycle* (New York: Basic Books, 1968).

This is a brilliantly written analysis of the current theories of developmental psychology, drawing on various schools such as that of Erik Erikson and Jean Piaget. Every reviewer commends it, and it is rapidly becoming the basic text in pastoral psychology. This is to say that if you have not read it, do so immediately.

PACKARD, VANCE. *Sexual Wilderness* (New York: David Mac-Kay, 1968).

The great value of this book is its review of the psychological and sociological research in the field and the author's rather moderate and considered judgments. It is the kind of book that is meant to capitalize on a public concern, and therefore is not particularly profound. We recommend that it be used as a source for data and not for a theological or philosophical orientation.

RUBIN, ISADORE. *Sexual Life After Sixty* (New York: Basic Books, 1968).

This is a somewhat technical volume that can be of great assistance to the clergy in counseling that growing portion of our population—those over sixty. It does a good job of doing away with much nonsense, commonly held, in a tasteful manner. It might be noted that it takes a rather neutral attitude as regards sexual outlets for widows and widowers.

SATIR, VIRGINIA. *Conjoint Family Therapy* (rev. ed.; Palo Alto, Calif.: Science and Behavior Books, 1967).

Not everything that has gone on at the Esalen Institute has made good sense, but Virginia Satir (no longer there) does. This is a basic book in the field, the kind of thing every family counselor ought to aspire to do well. Her method is built around a communication theory and the unverbalized needs people have for marriage. It is the single best book we knew for the priest/counselor to try to master.

THURIAN, MAX. *Marriage and Celibacy*. Trans. NORMA EMERTON (London: SCM Press, 1959). O.p.

A Protestant monk argues here for the option to the celibate life. His reasons include practical matters, those for the sake of the inner life, and then the witness to the eschatological Church. This can be read with interest in the light of chapter 1, "A Theology of Sex." (Secondhand copies are probably available from a dealer such as Blackwell, Oxford, England.)

WOOD, FREDERIC C., JR. *Sex and the New Morality* (New York: Association, 1968).

In many ways this book is an exposition of some of the things we can only "mention by title" in chapter 1. The author believes that the "new morality" provides a context for working out a pattern of creative sexual behavior, and he seeks to spell out what this might be. The whole thing is made very much alive by a series of case studies. The approach of the author is, as is now frequently true, person-centered.

GENERAL INTEREST BOOKS FOR ADULTS

Many of the books listed in the previous section can be read by the average layman with profit. However, those included in this section are more specifically related to the general questions of the layman.

BAILEY, D. S. *Common Sense About Sexual Ethics* (New York: Macmillan, 1962).

This is a popularization of the conclusions of one of the Church's leading theologians in this area. It is a solid little book of a more or less liberal bent as compared, say, to Demant's book (see below).

CAPON, ROBERT FARRAR. *Bed and Board* (New York: Simon & Schuster, 1965).

While his prejudices may not be quite ours in all instances (e.g., re birth control, modern architecture, and wine cellars), this is a thoroughly delightful book. It is a marvelous introduction to the art of being human in marriage. We would recommend it (with a couple of provisos) for distribution in premarital instruction along with *A Doctor Speaks on Sexual Expression in Marriage* (Hastings, see below).

DEMANT, VIGO AUGUSTE. *Christian Sex Ethics: An Introduction* (New York: Harper & Row, 1964).

This book embodies a rather conservative, academic approach (Bailey, see above). It consists of lectures delivered at Oxford. "We have now looked at four ways in which the love of man and woman has been thought of as a symbol of theological mysteries. . . . Marriage can be accepted and embraced as a high vocation only in a world in which there exists some feasible and proper alternative . . . marriage . . . as a full meeting of two whole persons is violated by venereal adventures before or outside marriage. . . . You can only appreciate fruitfully the good things of the world . . . if you don't trust them over much."

GINOTT, HAIM G. *Between Parent and Child* (New York: Macmillan, 1965).

This book probably deserves its wide reputation. Its overall view is solid and helpful; in fact, it is an extremely supportive book while at the same time a real judgment on our treatment of our children. Specifically, its discussion of sexuality and sex education seems to us very much in line with what we have offered here.

————. *Between Parent and Teenager* (New York: Macmillan, 1969).

Like many sequels, this book is not up to the original. The adolescent is a very complicated person, and we suspect the kind of treatment Dr. Ginott gives the child makes for some very superficial insights as to the adolescent. For example, to dismiss masturbation as essentially "self-centered" is not a responsible way of treating some very complicated feelings on the part of both parents and the teenager. We think the book is helpful, but we include it here only because we recommend his first book highly and assume that the reader would ask about the one on teenagers.

HANSEL, ROBERT R. *Like Father, Like Son—Like Hell!* (New York: Seabury, 1969).

It would be of considerable help to adults in dealing with the situation of youth today to understand more clearly just what the famous "gap" is all about. Rejecting all other labels, Fr. Hansel calls it an "assumption gap" and is convinced that it exists not only between the generations but between one group of young people and another, which he designates as "the settled" and "the searching." Read privately and perhaps followed by adult discussion, the book should provide an excellent basis for a thorough examination of parental attitudes. A reconsideration of these attitudes will contribute greatly to the good and open relationships required—above all—in the formation of valid sexual responses.

HASTINGS, DONALD W. *A Doctor Speaks on Sexual Expression in Marriage* (New York: Bantam Books, 1967).

This book, together with that by Capon (see above) is what we recommend for distribution to couples getting married. It is a frank, illustrated (including some line drawings of positions in coitus), discussion of how to do intercouse well. It is not a discussion of the meaning of love, nor does it discuss moral issues. It does benefit—as no other manual we know—from the Masters and Johnson research. We highly recommend it.

HETTLINGER, RICHARD F. *Living with Sex: The Student's Dilemma* (New York: Seabury, 1966).

This is an excellent book to be used with college-age people, either as a gift to one person or as a study guide. It has a sane, reasoned approach and explores the "why" of the Church's previous position, which is so obviously at variance with much of what the author now says. We have made several references to this book, indicating something of the author's opinions, in chapter 5.

RAINER, JEROME and JULIA. *Sexual Pleasure in Marriage* (New York: Simon & Schuster [Pocket Books], 1962).

This book is intended primarily for the married couple for whom sex is a bore, an isolated event for physical or psychological release, or simply a terror. Some pastors use it as a book to be distributed to premarital couples, but Hastings' book (see above) is better for this purpose. The Rainer work is quite explicit in matters such as oral-genital stimulation and other techniques for "putting the romance back in your sex life" and might best be reserved for those emotionally prepared for such recommendations.

RYAN, JOHN JULIAN and MARY PERKINS. *Love and Sexuality: A Christian Approach* (New York: Holt, Rinehart & Winston, 1967).

Written by an articulate, postconciliar, Roman Catholic couple, it discusses in a pleasant and readily understood manner many things to which we refer in this study. The authors are admirers of Robert Capon, but in some ways we think they are superior to him. Certainly they convey a profound sense of the human in life and at the same time embrace the gifts of modern behavioral and social science. Although they do not say so explicitly, it is clear that the authors are not in agreement with the teachings contained in *Humanae Vitae,* which document was issued after their book. We particularly recommend the chapter on "The Role of the Body in Human Relationships."

SIECUS Study Guides. #s1–7: "Sex Education," "Homosexuality," "Masturbation," "Characteristics of Male and Female Sexual Responses," "Premarital Sexual Standards," "Sexual Relations During Pregnancy and the Post-Delivery Period," and "Film Resources for Sex Education" (Sex Information and Education Council of the U.S., Inc. [Publications Office, 1825 Willow Rd., Northfield, Ill. 60093], 1965–68).

These are excellent studies issued in the cause of "sexual responsibility" in a pluralistic society. They are *not,* by intention or fact, pleas for any particular Christian morality. For example, in the area of premarital intercourse, the guide states: "The choice of a premarital sexual standard is a personal moral choice, and no amount of facts or trends can 'prove' scientifically that one ought to choose a particular standard." This statement seems to us incontrovertible and hardly advocating moral chaos.

BOOKS FOR YOUNG PEOPLE (JUNIOR AND SENIOR HIGH SCHOOL AGE)

These books are specifically intended for the 12–18 age bracket. Do not use any of them or the "Books for Children" (see below) without personal involvement as well.

DUVALL, EVELYN MILLIS. *Love and the Facts of Life* (New York: Association, 1963).

This is a revision of the standard work, *Facts of Life and Love for Teenagers.* It is the best work in the field to explain to the senior high teenager the physiological realities of human sexuality. The drawings, style, vocabulary, etc., are excellent. The author is not a Christian theologian, however she is a sane, mature woman. Note that there is a filmstrip that can be used with the book (see *Love and the Facts of Life*, under "Audio-Visual Aids," below).

———. *Why Wait Till Marriage?* (New York: Association, 1965).

This is the best treatment of the more obvious reasons for premarital chastity—fear of pregnancy, reputation, psychological guilt, etc. It destroys many of the old misconceptions used to rationalize many an experimentation. However, it is not *particularly* Christian in its approach, nor does it have the subtlety of Trobisch's book (see below).

JOHNSON, ERIC W. *Love and Sex in Plain Language* (rev. ed.; Philadelphia: Lippincott, 1967; New York: Bantam [Pathfinder], 1968).

This book is intended for the junior high adolescent, and it does its work very well. It deals explicitly with illustrations about the physiology of the sexual organs, coitus (in a brief and very tasteful manner), and even, in a very short chapter, heredity and the DNA molecule. It talks about the need for family planning and how it is done. Its best feature is the careful explanation of different rates of physical sexual maturing, important for the young teenager.

LEVINSOHN, FLORENCE and G. L. KELLY. *What Teenagers Want to Know* (Chicago: Budlong Press, 1965).

This book is in the same series as two others mentioned as such in "Books for Children" below. It is inexpensive and good, specific about physiological matters, and covers a wide area of psychological and social questions—everything from exercises for menstrual cramps to attitudes toward marrying.

LORAND, RHODA L. *Love, Sex and the Teenager* (New York: Macmillan, 1965).

The author is the wife of a famous psychiatrist and is a professional in the same general field. Her book contains good solid advice, based upon psychoanalytic theory. It covers a wider field than Duvall and goes deeper than Levinsohn. The format of the book might deter some teenagers from reading it (unlike Duvall). It *looks* dull. Some of her chapters include discussion of masculinity and femininity, masturbation, psychological first aid, getting along with parents, dating behavior, etc. It is a good book for parents to read as well. In our opinion, there is in it nothing particularly incompatible with the teaching of the Church. The author is certainly not "permissive," and she has recently come out against sex education in the elementary schools as currently being taught.

STRINGFELLOW, WILLIAM. *Instead of Death* (New York: Seabury, 1963).

A study course for young people to enable them to understand the meaning of "loneliness, sex, and the search for identity" in terms of the death and resurrection of our Lord. It can raise some good—if controversial—questions, about which young people ought to be thinking and to have the freedom to discuss in the Church.

TROBISCH, WALTER. *I Loved A Girl* (New York: Harper & Row, 1963).

Easily read in an hour or so, this is a collection of the correspondence between two young Africans and their Protestant pastor. It is probably the most eloquent testimony for premarital chastity available, though quite subtle. It would make good group study material. We recommend it highly.

BOOKS FOR CHILDREN (PRESCHOOL–JUNIORS)

We believe that the sex education of children should be principally *parental* and *in person*. Literature should only be supplemental. *Never* leave a book "just lying around to be discovered" by your child. We note below the supplemental material available that we recommend:

Budlong Press of Chicago has published a series of books (already mentioned; see Levinsohn, under "Books for Young People," above) *obtainable only through a doctor or priest*. We recommend the series without reservation as absolutely the best. The three books in the series relevant to children this age are:

LERRIGO, MARION O. and MICHAEL CASSIDY. *A Doctor Talks to 9- to 12-Year-olds* (Chicago: Budlong, 1964).

This carries the child through the history of human life, beginning with our biological heritage, through conception, pregnancy, and child birth. It also discusses the preteens. There is a section for parents that is to be removed and read before the book is given to the child. If there were any criticism, it would be that in our experience even an above average 9-year-old finds the book difficult going.

MEILACH, DONA Z. *A Doctor Talks to 5- to 8-Year-olds* (Chicago: Budlong, 1966).

This beautifully illustrated little book is excellent for its purpose. The principal theme explores the phenomena of reproduction in all of nature, including Man.

WARREN, S. L. and EDWARD B. ROSENBERG. *A Doctor Discusses the Pre-School Child's Learning Process and How Parents Can Help* (Chicago: Budlong, 1967).

This is intended for the reading of parents. It is good, solid, psychiatrically oriented material that assumes that infantile sexuality encompasses far more than genital activity. For example, it discusses the question: "Should my child learn to read early?" (The answer is a reasoned and gentle, "No!")

NEA and AMA together have published an inexpensive series of pamphlets on sex education that includes material for the child. The ones relating to this age are:

A Story About You (intended for 9–12-year-olds), 1964.

Parents' Responsibility (for parents of younger children to read), 1962.

They may be obtained from the American Medical Association, 535 N. Dearborn St., Chicago, Ill. 60610; or the National Education Association, 1201 Sixteenth St., N.W., Washington, D.C. 20036.

DUVALL, EVELYN MILLIS. *About Sex and Growing Up* (New York: Association, 1968).
This is a book for the preteen child, age 9–11, and is written in the usual frank, tactful Duvall style. It is illustrated by line drawings. There is no explicit description of sexual intercourse: "An egg alone cannot start a baby; it must be fertilized by a sperm from the father." There is a rather complete word list, although it is noteworthy that words such as "masturbation" are absent. Preteen problems, such as getting on with adults, having special friends, and controlling feelings, are discussed fully. It seems to us to be an excellent book for the end of childhood, just before puberty. A filmstrip, with the same name, that may be used with the book is noted in the "Audio-Visual Aids" listings, below.

LEVINE, MILTON I. and JEAN H. SELIGMANN. *A Baby Is Born: The Story of How Life Begins* (New York: Simon & Schuster [Golden], 1949).
This is for the young child, is an old standard, and is still excellent. The text is well done and the illustrations superb.

AUDIO-VISUAL AIDS

Audio-visual materials are never a substitute for *prepared leadership* and *personal dialogue*. They are only supportive of good teaching and should only be considered a tool. No audio-visual material should ever be used without (1) preview, (2) a clear idea of what it is intended to provoke or how it is intended to inform, and (3) ample opportunity for discussion following the viewing.

We would recommend to anyone interested in audio-visuals in this field that you obtain a copy of the Henk Newenhouse catalogue, "Sex Education and Family Living Materials" (Henk Newenhouse, Inc., 1825 Willow Rd., Northfield, Ill. 60093). This firm specializes in quality audio-visuals for sex education. However, once you discover something helpful in the catalogue, check with other distributors to see if you can obtain it at a cheaper rate. The Henk Newenhouse film rental prices are out of line. We also suggest consulting SIECUS Study Guide #7, "Film Resources for Sex Education," which lists a good number of 16mm films (see SIECUS listing, under "General Interest Books for Adults," above, for address). A subscription to the *Mass Media Ministries Bi-Weekly Newsletter* (2116 N. Charles St., Baltimore, Md. 21218) will keep you current with many audio-visuals, including films, filmstrips, flat pictures, records. Then it is also helpful to have the *Audio-Visual Resource Guide* available for evaluation of audio-visual resources. Previously published every two years, the *AVRG* has not been reissued since the 8th edition (1966; 597 pp.), but our information is that an updated issue is currently being planned by the publisher (National Council of Churches, 475 Riverside Dr., New York, N.Y. 10027).

The AVs we recommend here are simply those with which we are familiar or which we have had recommended to us by a reliable source. Addresses of producers and/or distributors noted for these lists are given at the end of this section.

"About Sex and Growing Up." 5-filmstrip series, with 5 study guides and 3 records. Produced by Cathedral Films. Sale, $45.00 a set.

The titles in this filmstrip series (which was produced to go with the book by the same title by Evelyn Duvall; see listing under "Books for Children," above), are: *Maturing Boys and*

Girls; *Become a Woman*; *Becoming a Man*; *Where Babies Come From*, and *Creation, Sex, and Faith*. The filmstrips consist of colored drawings. As are the other Duvall audio-visuals (see below), this series is well done. Until recently it was the only acceptable material of its kind for 9- to 11-year-olds. Now it must be compared with *Life, Love, Sex . . . and You!* (see listing, below). Unlike material from Guidance Associates (e.g., see "Family Life and Sex Education" filmstrip series, below)— which is generally technically superior, but which does not provide any material for this age group)—it is not associated with SIECUS. Some may consider this an advantage. Properly used, the "About Sex and Growing Up" filmstrip series can contribute to the sex education of children in the 9–11 age bracket.

"*A Basis for Sex Morality.*" 6-filmstrip series, color, script, seven study guides, records. Produced by Cathedral Films. Available through most church audio-visual libraries. Sale, about $45.00 a set.

These filmstrips (they are lectures, with visual illustrations, presented by the Rev. Canon Bryan Green to college students; see discussion on p. 109) are entitled: *Love, Friendship, and Marriage*; *The Nature of Sex*; *The Man–Woman Relationship*; *Pre-Marital Relationships*; *Rationalizing Sex Behavior*, and *Guidelines for Sex Behavior*. Each lasts 18 min. except #1 (17 min.) and #4 (14 min.) The accompanying records may or may not be used. *AVRG* highly recommends the series *for discussion* with senior high through young adults.

Boy to Man and *Girl to Woman*. Two 16mm color films, each 16 min. Produced as companion films by Churchill Films. Widely available from university and other educational film libraries and distributors (e.g., from Henk Newenhouse at $17.00 each).

Both films are well-done presentations of development at puberty, which can be used profitably with children in the 12– 14 age bracket. Boys and girls should see both films in order to understand each other's problems. Where this has been done we know the results to have been excellent.

Life, Love, Sex . . . and You! 8-filmstrip series, with records and resource guide. Produced and sold by the Thomas S. Klise Co. $110 a set.

The titles of the filmstrips are: *Love Makes the World Go Round*; *Love Gives Life*; *It's Great to be a Boy*; *Getting to be a Man*; *It's Great to be a Girl*; *Becoming a Woman*; *Your Heredity, Your Environment, and You*, and *Your Life Today Determines Your Future*. They are intended for children age 10–12, which means they should be compared with the Duvall series, "About Sex and Growing Up" (see above). In this regard, they seek to explore the broader concept of sexuality not found in the other material, as well as to overcome the "latent puritanism" of which Mrs. Duvall can be guilty. Klise's filmstrips are becoming well known for their creative use of artwork and their insightful employment of contemporary theology. This particular set is advertised for use *with parents*, which should overcome some possible objections. We highly recommend it.

Especially for Boys. 47-frame, color filmstrip, with record, guide. Produced by Wexler Film Productions. Sale, by Henk Newenhouse, $15.00.

This is a well-done presentation on reproduction for boys age 10–12. It has creative and colorful contemporary artwork and is natural and frank.

Family Life and Sex Education. Filmstrip series with 31 titles (sets), each covering one to four filmstrips (one title consists of 80 slides), with records, teacher's manual. Produced by Guidance Associates, in cooperation with a special committee of SIECUS (but not published by SIECUS).

This series is by all means the best thing out, and neither we nor any reviewer whose mature judgment we trust finds anything in the filmstrips objectionable. They have been the subject of much controversy as a result of extreme right-wing attacks on SIECUS. The photography and drawing is arresting, the sound (including music) is superb, and the content is excellent. The series is expensive, and the kind of thing only a very large parish or diocesan library can afford to buy. The sets for each title run between $20.00 and $45.00, with one as high as $70.00. The free catalogue from Guidance Associates lists the many titles (including *Masculinity and Femininity*); we strongly urge you to order it.

From Generation to Generation. 16mm, color film, 30 min. Produced by the Maternity Center Association in 1959. Available from Audio-Visual Library, Executive Council of the Episcopal Church (rental, $12.00) and most state Departments of Health.

This is a beautiful film, placing human reproduction in the context of all life. It is reverently done, with excellent technical skill. We recommend it highly for junior highs and up.

The Game. 16mm, b&w film, 28 min. Produced by the National Film Board of Canada. Free loan through the Canadian Consulate; rental from Henk Newenhouse, $17.00; from Mc-Graw-Hill/Contemporary Films, $8.00.

An outstanding film, it deals with the theme of boy–girl relationships—centering on a premarital sex episode—from the boy's viewpoint. Open-ended, it demands discussion as a followup. We recommend it highly for senior highs and up.

How Babies Are Made. 44-frame filmstrip, with record (or 44 slides) in color, with teacher's guide. Originated by Creative Scope, Inc. Produced by and available from General Learning Corp.

Designed for use with children 5–8 in conjunction with *A Doctor Talks to 5- to 8-Year-Olds* (see listing under "Books for Children," above). It shows, in a series of animated cartoons, animal and human reproduction, including coitus (with the human mother and father covered up to the armpits by bedding). It is not the kind of material to use without consulting parents. It would be better used by parents with their own children. Some of the controversy about sex education in elementary schools has been apparently focused on indiscriminate use of this series.

Human Reproduction. 16mm, color film, revised in 1965, running time 21 min. Produced by McGraw-Hill/Contemporary Films. Available from producer and many state libraries. Rental, about $20.00.

This is a factual, objective presentation of the subject, and it includes models, animated drawings, and a live scene in a delivery room. It is the film used in *Fit to Be Tied* (see pp. 109, 110). Its goal is objective familiarity with the facts of human reproduction. Highly recommended by *AVRG* for junior and senior highs.

Love and the Facts of Life. 6-filmstrip series, about 57 frames each, color, with records, scripts, guides. Produced by Cathedral Films.

Based on Dr. Evelyn Millis Duvall's well-known book of the same name (see listing under "Books for Young People," above), it examines questions of sex in the context of one's total life experience. It has contemporary artwork, with frank portrayals. It even shows an erection. The titles of the six strips are: *Learning About Love and Sex*; *Growing Up, From Childhood to Maturity*; *Having a Baby*; *Understanding Your Love Feelings*; *Who Am I?: The Search for Self*; and *Sex and Your Religious Faith*. Strip #5 has a section on contraception. Recommended for junior and senior highs and their parents. We found that with some more sophisticated students, however, use of these filmstrips hindered discussion more than helped. The series is not identified with SIECUS, which may be a virtue in some situations.

The Merry-Go-Round (do not confuse with *Signposts on a Merry-Go-Round*). 16mm, b&w film, 23 min. Produced by National Film Board of Canada, 1966. Available from McGraw-Hill/Contemporary Films. Rental, $6.00.

This is a discussion of adolescent views on sex by three people: Ann Landers, Mary Winspear (a school principal), and Albert Ellis. The subject is controversial and the positions diverse. It *must* be followed by discussion, and it is highly recommended for senior highs and adults if it is.

A Normal Birth. 16 mm, b&w film, 11 min. Produced and distributed by Medical Arts Production, Inc. Available from Henk Newenhouse. Rental, $10.00.

This is a literal photographic record of a childbirth, with good commentary, and requiring discussion afterwards. If you have a need to show how it happens, this is the best thing available for senior highs and up.

Phoebe: Story of a Premarital Pregnancy. 16mm, b&w film, 29 min. Produced by National Film Board of Canada. Available through McGraw-Hill/Contemporary Films. Rental, $8.00.

Ostensibly, this is the story of a teenage girl's difficulty in telling her boyfriend and her parents that she is pregnant. To describe it this way does not begin to explain the profundity and power of this film. All kinds of questions can arise from its viewing, and we consider it the most provocative aid of its kind for teenage discussion of questions vital to them. We recommend it highly for senior highs and up.

To Plan Your Family. 16 mm, color film, 14 min. Produced by Churchill Films. Available from Henk Newenhouse. Rental, $15.00.

This film seeks to persuade women of limited education of the need for family planning and to explain to them through animated drawings how it can be done. The film especially advocates the pill and the inter-uterine device.

A Guide to Audio-Visual Aids by Age Groups

- 6–8: *How Babies Are Made* (34 slides)
- 9–11: *"About Sex and Growing Up"* (4-filmstrip series)
  Especially for Boys (filmstrip)
  "Life, Love, Sex . . . and You!" (8-filmstrip series)
- 12–14: *Boy to Man* and *Girl to Woman* (2 films)
  Some of *"Family Life and Sex Education"* (31-title filmstrip/slide series)
  From Generation to Generation (film)
  Human Reproduction (film)
  "Love and the Facts of Life" (6-filmstrip series)
- 15–18: All in the 12–14 age bracket
  A Basis for Sex Morality (6-filmstrip series)
  Most of *"Family Life and Sex Education"* (31-title filmstrip/slide series)
  The Merry-Go-Round (film)
  A Normal Birth (film)
  Phoebe (film)
  The Game (film)
- Adults: All in the 12–14 and 15–18 age brackets.
  All of *"Family Life and Sex Education"* (31-title filmstrip/slide series)
  To Plan Your Family (film)